Daniel V. Lucas

Australia and Homeward

Daniel V. Lucas

Australia and Homeward

ISBN/EAN: 9783337311711

Printed in Europe, USA, Canada, Australia, Japan

Cover: Foto ©ninafisch / pixelio.de

More available books at **www.hansebooks.com**

AUSTRALIA

AND

HOMEWARD.

BY

REV. D. VANNORMAN LUCAS, M.A.

TORONTO:
WILLIAM BRIGGS, 78 & 80 KING STREET EAST.
MONTREAL: C. W. COATES.   HALIFAX: S. F. HUESTIS.
1888.

Entered, according to Act of the Parliament of Canada, in the year one thousand eight hundred and eighty-eight, by DANIEL VANNORMAN LUCAS, in the Office of the Minister of Agriculture, at Ottawa.

TO

MY FELLOW-SOLDIER IN FIGHTING LIFE'S BATTLES,

MY FELLOW-VOYAGER OVER

THE GREAT OCEANS,

AND

MY FELLOW-TRAVELLER IN MANY LANDS,

My Wife,

THIS VOLUME IS RESPECTFULLY AND LOVINGLY

DEDICATED.

INTRODUCTION.

THIS book was written almost entirely at sea. I should have been glad if I could have availed myself of more help from reliable and experienced authors.

I have given the names of those whose writings have been of service to me, and whose valuable works I fortunately had with me.

Much that I have written of the natives, animals, birds, and of the country, is the result of personal observation. The reader, I think, will see that I must have taken a deep interest in everything pertaining to the home of our antipodean friends, who are not only like ourselves, a Christian people, but descendants from the same stock, and fellow-subjects of the same great Empire, and, equally with us, admirers of, and loyal to, Her Most Gracious Majesty Queen Victoria.

Perhaps in no other part of Her Majesty's wide domain has there been such rapid progress in agriculture, arts, education, and all other things embraced by the term "national prosperity."

INTRODUCTION.

I have, first of all, given the reader some account (a very brief one) of the aborigines, and then have described, in natural order, the animals, birds, and native trees and flowers, before referring to the new race who have, by their superior knowledge, wrought such wonders in that vast island-continent within the last half century.

The continent of Australia is, in round numbers, 2,500 miles from East to West, and 2,000 miles from North to South. It is divided into New South Wales, Queensland, Victoria, South Australia, and West Australia. These embrace a little over 3,000,000 square miles of territory.

The term Australasia includes the continent of Australia, and the islands of New Zealand, Tasmania, and other smaller adjacent islands as well.

D. V. L.

CONTENTS.

AUSTRALIA AND THE AUSTRALIANS.

	PAGE
THE AUSTRALIAN NATIVES	9
THE AUSTRALIAN ANIMALS	61
THE AUSTRALIAN BIRDS	75
THE FLORA OF AUSTRALIA	104
SIGNS OF PROGRESS	112
MELBOURNE COFFEE PALACES	130
BURKE AND WILLS, THE EXPLORERS	145
PERILS OF PIONEERING	151

AUSTRALIA AND HOMEWARD.

FIRST LETTER............ 187
    Celebrating a Local Option Victory in Melbourne—Farewell Address—Lecture at Hamilton—Visit Ararat—Lecture at Stawell—Christmas in Adelaide with the Thermometer at 95° in the shade—Address a Christmas Sabbath-school gathering—On board the *Massilia*—Painful Death of a Passenger—King George's Sound.

SECOND LETTER............ 196
    The Ship's Physician a Canadian—Composition of the Ship's Crew—Mohammedans preferred because they are Pledged Teetotallers—Watches at Sea—Monotony of a Landsman's Life at Sea—"Man Overboard!"

CONTENTS.

	PAGE
THIRD LETTER	204

Arrival in Ceylon—Preaching in the "Oldest Wesleyan Chapel in Asia"—Burial Place of Rev. Dr. Coke—Forms of Religion in Ceylon—Buddhism and Brahminism compared—Population of Ceylon—Mohammedans attending the Wesleyan College—Printing and Publishing Establishment—Conversions to Christianity—Labors of a Native Preacher.

FOURTH LETTER 214

Progress of Christianity in Ceylon—Importance of Ceylon to Britain as the "Key to India"—Prosperity under British Rule—Roads as Educators.

FIFTH LETTER 221

Burying a Babe at Sea—Socotra Island—Arabian Traders—Arabian Divers—The Red Sea.

SIXTH LETTER 228

Dangers to Navigation in the Red Sea—Suez—Sinai Peninsula and its Heart-moving Memories—Tel-el-Kebir—Pyramids and Sphinx—Cairo—Mosque of Mohamed Ali.

SEVENTH LETTER 246

Alexandria—The Adriatic—Brindisi—Naples—Vesuvius—Pompeii—Puzzoli and the Appian Way—Rev. F. Sciarelli—Rev. Salvatore Ragghiante—Reform in Italy.

EIGHTH LETTER 260

Rome—The Catacombs—The Sistine Chapel—Michael Angelo and Raphaelo—The Pantheon—The Corso.

NINTH LETTER 269

The Arch of Titus—Roman Coliseum—Lines on the Coliseum, by Clarence Lucas—The Home of the Cæsars—The Holy Stairs—Signs of the Times in Italy.

TENTH LETTER 278

The World my Parish—Armadia—Great Florentines—Art in Florence—Milan Cathedral.

ELEVENTH LETTER 284

Switzerland—Winter in the Alps—Paris—From Calais to Dover.

TWELFTH LETTER—LONDON 292

The Tower of London—Epping Forest—"Hunting Lodge" of "Good Queen Bess"—Growth of London—A Stroll—The Nelson Column—The London Law Courts—St. Paul's Cathedral—The Fore Leg of a Horse—A "Beef-eater"—Princess Elizabeth's Prison in the Bell Tower—Block and Headsman's Mask—Billingsgate—Thames Embankment—Houses of Parliament—Parks—Westminster Abbey—Windsor Castle—Handel Musical Festival—London Thieves.

Australia and the Australians.

THE AUSTRALIAN NATIVES.

THEIR ORIGIN.

MR. CURR shows by quotations from Dr. Livingstone, Rev. Duff Macdonald and others, the wonderful resemblance between the Australian natives and the negroes of Africa, in manners and customs, and argues from this that they are of one common origin.

Their systems of witchcraft, the admittance of adult males to the rights of manhood through the medium of mysterious and very cruel ceremonies; the facts relating to marriage, the customs respecting burials; the singular practice of mutual avoidance between son-in-law and mother-in-law, the dread of hair falling into the hands of an enemy, the mode of tossing water into the mouth, and several other similar customs, from which it would appear that both peoples, far apart as Africa and Australia are, have originally learned all these things from the same source.

Besides the above, many words used by the Australians are apparently, at least, of the same root as words used by the Africans to express the same ideas.

Such words as *woman, breasts, milk, mother, water, rain, mouth, tongue, eat, drink* are all traceable to the same root-words whence words meaning the same thing in Africa seem to have come.

There are, however, notwithstanding these resemblances, differences in other respects, which almost render it impossible for the reader to assign to the two peoples a common origin.

The African is a sooty black; the Australian has, while black, a coppery tint. The hair of the negro is scant in quantity and *woolly* in texture, while that of the Australian is most abundant, and straight or wavy—never woolly.

As a rule, the negro is almost entirely devoid of beard and whiskers, while the native of the island-continent is abundantly supplied with both; so that it may be said that the negro is one of the least and the Australian one of the most hairy of men, as our picture of one of them, on the opposite page, will show.

There is a strong probability in favor of the hypothesis that the differences between the two have resulted from a cross of blood. For the reasons given above, " there seems to be no room to doubt," says Mr.

AUSTRALIAN NATIVE.

Curr, "that the Australian is, by descent, a Negro, with a strong cross in him of some other race; but of what race I have found no evidence to show."

They are far from being as fine a race of men as our North American aborigines. During our stay of nearly a year in Australia, we saw many of them, both at the mission stations and elsewhere, but none of them were above five feet ten inches in height, and it was very rare to see one above five feet eight.

We visited the schools, and from the quickness displayed by some of the little black fellows, and from what we saw of those that were older, together with statements made by writers, such as Mr. Curr, Mr. Dawson and others, we cannot but regard them as having a fair intellectual capacity. Mr. Curr says: "The children at the stations learn reading, writing and arithmetic more easily than white children; and if their education is persevered in for several generations, I see no reason to prevent their being brought, in this particular, to a level with ourselves."

I have seen a letter written by a native aboriginal girl which would reflect credit upon any girl of her age, no matter what may have been her birthplace or parentage.

She was a pupil at Mr. Camfield's school, King George's Sound.

"ANNESFIELD HOUSE,
March 5, 1866.

"MY DEAR MRS. MITCHELL,—I thank you very much for the beautiful cake you sent me. When it arrived on Wednesday afternoon Mrs. Camfield did not know who it was for, until she read Anne Courthope's letter, and then she found that it was for me.

"Mr. Camfield said that he was jealous that it was not for him. I must thank you for the pretty needle-book that came with Miss Trimmer. She arrived on Saturday, 3rd.

"Last month a ship came from Adelaide with two thousand eight hundred and fifty sheep in it. They looked so pretty.

"Three days afterward they went eleven miles. They kicked up such a dust going along. The road runs past our paddock.

"Mr. Camfield was delighted with the pretty watch bags and the garters; he said they were the very things he wanted.

"The doll that was sent for Louisa Mrs. Camfield gave it to Tela, because she has not had one, and Louisa has had three or four. Louisa is so fond of Mr. Mitchell, she helped him yesterday to pick up the apples.

"I have no more to say, my dear Mrs. Mitchell, so I must conclude with best love to yourself.

"I am your grateful
"BESSY FLOWER."

Mr. Smith, in his large and interesting work on the

ORIGIN OF AUSTRALIAN NATIVES. 15

aborigines of Victoria, says: "In talking to a clever Australian native, one feels that he is speaking to a person who has all the faculties (though undeveloped) of a European. Such a native is quiet and dignified in his manner."

LANGUAGES.

Mr. Curr, in his exhaustive work, gives specimens of over two hundred distinct languages, and suggests that the real number will probably approach nearer to five hundred. By this I presume he means to include some that might more properly be termed mere dialects.

To show the reader how widely these languages differ, I have compiled from Mr. Curr's tables, and have rearranged, several words with the equivalents, as spoken by tribes from different parts of the Australian continent, as specimens.

Let us take, *e.g.*, the words *kangaroo, opossum, a young man, baby.*

Name of Tribe.	Kangaroo.	Opossum.	Young Man.	Baby.
Port Darwin.	Langootpa	Macmilla.	Mullenjiu.	Larree.
Raffles Bay.	Ieepoogee.	Mungulan.	Ominamun	Geelarak.
Gudang Tribe.	Ipamoo.	Omara.	Ipunga.	Ingara.
The Ngurla Tribe.	Mungaroo.	Wallumbene	Bukali.	Mulgani.

NAME OF TRIBE.	KANGAROO.	OPOSSUM.	YOUNG MAN.	BABY.
Nickol Bay.	Mungarro.	Wolumberree	Buckalle.	Gumbarra.
Shark's Bay.	Yowerda.	Yoorda.	Wiabandy.	Yamba.
Champion Bay.	Yooada.	Waiada.	Agarthar.	Nurelee.
Minnal Yungar Tribe	Yankera.	Koomal.	Mundey.	Kullang.
Murchison River.	Yowardoo.	Widdra.	Marroowa.	Kogga.
Muliarra Tribe.	Marloo.	Wyadoo.	Athugari.	Jura
Natigero Tribe.	Bikkut.	Wykooter.	Thukkaree	
Warrangoo Tribe.	Yungur.	Koomal.	Weerbindy	Kooning.
Eucla Tribe.	Madooroo.	Bilda.	Majilba.	Walboo
Macumba River.	Uggerra.	Andinua.	Wedea.	Uccachea.
Gawler Range.	Kurdloo.	Pilla.	Ooltapa.	Poolyoo.
Cooper's Creek.	Thaldara.	Murrathurra	Bulcabitthee.	Warniwah

From the language of the Dieyerie tribe we have the verb "to love" conjugated by Mr. S. Gason, who resided among them for nine years. According to his testimony it is little they know of love, for he says: "A more treacherous race I do not believe exists. They imbibe treachery in their infancy and practise it till death, and have no sense of wrong in it." And you would, dear reader, love little if you had to do it after this fashion:

      I am loving—Athoogoorana.
      Thou art loving—Yondrooyoorana.
      He is loving—Noolieayoorana.
      We are loving—Uldrayoorana.

You are loving—Yinieyoorana.
They are loving—Thanayoorna.

I had loved—Athooyooranaori.
Thou hadst loved—Yondrooyooranawonthie.
He had loved—Nooleayooranawonthie.
We had loved—Uldrayooranawonthie.
You had loved—Yinieyooranawonthie.
They had loved—Thanayooranawonthie.

The following is from the conjugation of the same word in the Pine Plain, North Wimmera language:

    I love—Goongeenon.
    Thou lovest—Goongeen
    He loves—Goongeena.
    We love—Goongeenan.
    You love—Goongeenat.
    They love—Goongenatt.

I shall have loved—Goongeengnanon mala.
Thou wilt have loved—Goongeengnona mala.
He will have loved—Goongeengnanan mala.
We shall have loved—Goongeenango malano.
You shall have loved—Goongeenang malano.
They shall have loved—Goongenango malano.

Some sentences, showing the idiom of their language, may be interesting:—

A kangaroo is feeding in the scrub. Native—*There kangaroo is feeding thick one scrub.*

Get me my spear and I will kill him. Native—*Hand me here my spear; him kill I will.*

I am going to sharpen my spear. Native—*To sharpen, going am I my spear.*

I am going to pour out the water. Native—*To pour out going am I the water.*

I am going to watch him. Native—*To watch him going am I.*

NOTATION.

Their only words for numerals are:

        One—Coornoo.
        Two—Mundroo.
        Three—Paracoola.

When they desire to express a greater number, they add together the words given above.

Four—Mundro-la, mundro-la.

Five—Mundroo, mundroo, coornoo; that is, twice 2 and 1.

Six—Mundroo-la, mundroo-la, mundroo-la; that is, thrice 2.

Ten—Mundroo-la, five times repeated. After ten, to twenty, the term murrathidna, from murra (hands), and thidna (feet), is used, and the fingers and toes are brought into requisition. After twenty, they show by signs that it is a great many, an innumerable quantity, for at twenty their arithmetic is exhausted.

As elsewhere, it is very common for white men to give native names to places, or retain names of rivers and mountains, such as the natives had themselves given them, prior to the white man's advent. We find in many of these the custom among the natives of repeating a word or a sound, to give force or emphasis to the idea. For instance, the river which flows through Melbourne is the *Yarra-Yarra—flowing, flowing;* that is, *ever* flowing. Other streams may go dry, but this, *never.*

I found, in travelling largely through the country, many places named according to this rule: *Bet-Bet, Gerong-Gerung, Buln-Buln, Burrum-Burrum.* This last is the name of a parish, and signifies *very muddy;* that is, *muddy, muddy.*

At Sydney we saw on the 'bus the name *Wooloomooloo*, the native name of a suburb of that city. I thought that the white people had purposely and unnecessarily given the name that orthography, but I found, on looking into the peculiarities of the language, that it could not be otherwise spelled and convey a correct native sound to the ear, for, while the sound of *u* enters very largely into their language, it has always with them the same sound as our *oo*.

Their love of reduplication is seen more in their names of mountains, rivers or places than in the names of persons or in common conversation. Take the native names of mountains for illustration: Mittagong, Tumanwong, Gullongalong, Warrawolong, Poppong, Wollungong, Cunglebung, Trunbarumba, Nackie-Nackie, Nurrumbidjee, Wagga-Wagga, Goonoo-Goonoo, Gooloogong.

CHILDREN.

When a native child is born it is as white as a European child. Some writers say that it will become black in about two weeks, others say they are from two to eight years old before they become thoroughly black. Like the men who disputed respecting the color of the chameleon, both are right, I presume. Little boys of five or six years sometimes have as much hair on the cheeks as a European of seventeen.

The child is usually nursed for a much longer period than is done with white people. Infanticide is universal. Whether it is largely practised or not depends altogether upon the ease or difficulty with which food can be procured for the tribe. Children are not supposed to have souls before they are five years old.

At a very early age the child must begin to seek

food for itself. The father instructs it in the art of digging for the larvæ of insects and grubs. He teaches it also how to catch fish, throw the boomerang and the toy spear.

Children are never chastised. They are simply kept under control, so far as they are controlled at all, by superstitious dread. Such and such things, they are told, will happen if they do so and so.

The first-born child, if not destroyed, is named after the parent, father or mother, as the case may be. After that, children are named after some animal which may happen near at the time—kangaroo, emu, dog, rat, or the like; or perhaps after something in the immediate locality of its birth—tree, pond, or lake.

A native was named Ber-uke (kangaroo-rat), one of these animals having crossed the floor of the hut about the time of his birth.

Poleeorong (cherry-tree) was so named because he was born under a cherry-tree. *Weing-paru* (fire and water), because the hut took fire, which was extinguished by water.

Girls are often named after flowers. People often exchange names; not, however, until they have been permitted to do so by the great council.

When one dies, his name is not mentioned while the

days of mourning last, which, with some tribes, are prolonged several months.

To call the name during these days is regarded as an insult to the deceased. If the deceased has borne the name of an animal, bird, or flower, such an object must be called by some other name during these months. Take, for instance, a case where the dead person has had the name *Waa* (crow).

During the days of mourning, it would not do to give the bird that name, lest thereby you pronounce the name of the dead. For the time being, by all mourning friends the bird is called not *waa*, but *narrapart*.

The black cockatoo (wilan) is called *waang*, the black snake, *mowang*, is called *kundereetch*.

A considerable confusion is occasioned by this strange superstition. The name given the child is not the one by which he will be known in after life When he is admitted to manhood rank in his tribe, he receives an entirely new name; and if his career should be marked by any striking event, he will then receive a name more worthy of him, and his old name will entirely disappear. Nicknames are often given, and the natives are said to be very happy in their effort to choose names that aptly describe eccentricities, peculiarities of face or ways of walking or speaking. Many very cruel ceremonies are observed before the young man is entitled to be ranked as a man or to receive his full permanent designation.

Two of his front teeth must be knocked out; the cartilage of his nose must be pierced; in some tribes his hair is pulled out by the roots; he must be circumcised and tatooed, or have his skin sometimes on his back, sometimes on his arms, or his face scarified or cut, and the skin raised and clay or charcoal shoved in so that when it heals, the skin will, at those places, be higher than that which has not been injured. These marks are supposed to add beauty to the person's appearance, and the young gentleman is very proud of them.

The only mutilation of females is the amputation of one, or sometimes two, joints of the little finger. They pretend to say that this finger will be in her way when she comes to wind her thread for making nets and knitting bags.

MARRIAGE.

A young man cannot marry till he is initiated into manhood rank by ceremonies which are in some tribes very cruel. Occasionally a weak young man is killed outright. If he survive, however, he is taken away for some months to a neighboring friendly tribe, where he is very tenderly cared for. When he returns he is introduced to his intended wife.

Considerable preparations are made. Emus' and swans' eggs, opossums, kangaroos, and wild fowls are cooked. The bride is adorned with an opossum rug; emu feathers are about her loins. Her hair is braided and bound about with a brow-band of plaited bark. The bridegroom is similarly adorned. Both are painted with white streaks over and under their eyes. In some tribes he is attended by two or three bachelors, who lead him to his bride, who receives him with downcast eyes. He then declares that he receives her as his wife, and feasting begins.

In other tribes, I find, the father leads the woman to the hut of her intended husband, and she kindles a fire for him, which completes the ceremony.

There is a custom which prevails throughout all the tribes, which would, perhaps, be an advantage if practised by some persons in civilized countries. The mother-in-law cannot, under any circumstances, speak to her daughter's husband, not even if he were dying. " When a girl has been promised to a man in marriage, or when he is married, the man and the mother of his wife, or betrothed, scrupulously avoid each other."

The Rev. E. Fuller, missionary at Fraser's Island, says, in an account he gives of his mission:

"The mother-in-law must not look upon her son-in-law at any time; they believe that if she did he would go mad, and would go and live in the bush like a wild man; when they all come together to sing at school time, there is great covering of heads by those women who may happen to have sons-in-law there, and you will see them 'backing' into their places in a most laughable manner, while the son-in-law will roll himself up in his blanket, or hide himself in some other way."

The natives have been often questioned respecting this custom, but they cannt tell why it exists, or when it began.

FURNITURE AND COOKING.

Their furniture is a very simple affair indeed.

Their baskets are made of rushes or bark of the acacia tree.

Their water buckets are made by sewing together a sheet of acacia bark. When it dries it assumes a circular shape.

Then they have millstones, mortars made of gray slate or marble. They carry for fire eucalyptus bark alight. Kindling a fire is a matter of considerable importance. If, in travelling, they cannot succeed in keeping their coals of eucalyptus alight, a good deal of time is lost in getting fire by friction. Where this is necessary, however, they have with them implements of various kinds for this purpose. Several modes are given to show how the native goes to work to obtain fire where he may have failed to bring with him from the last camping place. Of fire caused by lightning they have so superstitious a dread that they will not

A NATIVE AUSTRALIAN PRODUCING
FIRE BY FRICTION.

avail themselves of it, or venture near, as the demon which produced it is supposed to be lurking about not far off.

Among their legends the following is found:

Common fire belonged to the crows, who would not spare a light. The " fire-tailed " wren seeing the crows playing, by throwing lighted sticks about, stole a brand.

OTHER MODES OF OBTAINING FIRE.

A hawk took the fire-stick, and with it set the whole forest on fire. Since then there is plently of fire for light.

They have no idea of cooking anything by boiling. All their cooked food is either broiled or roasted.

They have, for cooking purposes, real old-fashioned ovens. When an opossum is killed the skin is *singed* off at once, then he is drawn, and roasted whole. In this way the meat is kept juicy for a much longer time when they are travelling. In these ovens they also roast kangaroos' tails, emus, wombats, turkeys, bear, wild dog, porcupine, flying squirrel, eagles, geese, swans, ducks, frogs, lizards and grubs. The grub is, with the Australian native, a great luxury.

Some specimens which we saw are quite four inches long, and nearly as large around as one's little finger.

In the cooking of fish they sometimes employ the following method: "A piece of thick and tender bark is selected and torn into an oblong form. The fish is laid in this, and the bark wrapped around it. Strings made from grass are then tied tightly about the bark and fish, which is then slowly baked in heated sand covered with hot ashes. When it is completed, the bark is opened, and serves as a dish. It is, of course, full of gravy and juice, not a drop of which has escaped. The fish cooked in this way is most delicious.

Ordinarily, fish are cooked by being thrown on the fire and broiled."

CANOES.

Their canoes are mostly made of bark. Usually the craft, which is very frail, consists of but one piece.

NATIVES' CANOES.

With a bit of pipe-clay or soft stone the native marks out the pattern on the side of a large tree. Then with his tomahawk he cuts along the mark, and **strips the bark from the tree.** The aid of fire is brought in to secure the desired shape. With tough hide, or sinews from the kangaroo, he sews up the ends, which he also plasters with mud or gums. If he is in a hurry, and if it is at that season of the year when the bark peels easily, a very good canoe can be constructed in an hour. Considerably more time than this is, however, usually taken.

It is very seldom, indeed, that Australian natives make any other than bark canoes. The bark of the red gum, the white gum, or blue gum, or almost any other kind of eucalyptus, is chosen.

The woods of Australia are much more difficult to work than the woods of America, being harder, closer grained, and more gnarled. Besides, the natives are far from loving anything that implies hard work.

WEAPONS.

The principal weapon is the spear. Some of those intended for war are eight or nine feet long, and weigh about four pounds. Some of these have barbs extending a foot or so back from the point, others are jagged with sharp flints or pieces of quartz fastened into grooves with gum.

For the chase they have much lighter spears, generally thrown with the aid of the *wommera*, an instrument very much resembling in shape a lady's crochet-needle. The point of the barb of the wommera rests in the end of the spear handle, the two lying parallel in the hand of the thrower, the spear lying between the upper part of the thumb and the fore-finger, while the wommera is gripped tightly between the knuckles of the fore and large fingers. By the use of this instrument he is able to continue to apply his force to his spear for a second or so longer than if thrown by the unaided hand only, and so can hurl it a greater distance.

Heavy spears, thrown seventy feet or more, seldom do any harm, as an enemy easily dodges them.

The heavy spear is often employed by the natives for killing the emu. The hunter ascends a tree near a drinking place, and as the bird passes underneath on its way to water, the spear is plunged into its back.

Making and pointing spears is a work of great labor. The native seldom throws his spear except when actually fighting or hunting. His dexterity is acquired by his constant throwing of toy spears in his youthful sports.

The most remarkable instrument used by Australian natives is the *boomerang*. This weapon is in shape like a scimitar. There are two kinds; the kind best known has the peculiarity of returning to the thrower, if it fails to hit the object at which it is thrown. How this effect is produced is to me a mystery. After having been projected horizontally fifty or even one hundred yards, it suddenly rises high into the air, and, revolving on its axis, with great speed returns to the point whence it was started. However, as a general rule, it hits the duck or other game, and so falls directly to the ground.

We found at one of the mission stations which we visited, where old customs had been discarded and the tribe had become thoroughly civilized, no one knew how to throw the boomerang. Though one handsome fellow, as black as a coal, made several attempts, for our sakes, he could not succeed. We were, for the time-being, considerably disappointed. We learned from it, however, that there is a skill that must be acquired even for throwing a boomerang.

Let would-be wits make note, lest their own unskilled jokes, failing to injure those aimed at, may rebound with greater force upon themselves.

The other kind of boomerang is longer and heavier. It is used more than the lighter sort in war and in the chase.

The wounds it inflicts are very severe.

Pointed sticks, very heavy at the pointed end, are used also in hunting. These are usually about two feet long. The natives are very expert at throwing

34 AUSTRALIA AND THE AUSTRALIANS.

these. We brought with us, on our return, a couple of these missiles, as also two or three boomerangs, some of which had seen service as pagan instruments of destruction.

The most useful of all instruments to the native is his tomahawk, or hatchet. Its head is a hard stone,

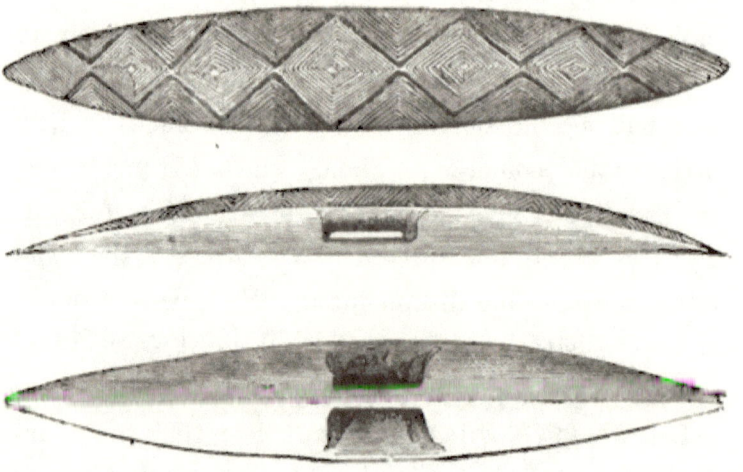

SHIELDS USED BY THE NATIVES.

which must be reduced to proper shape by knocking off flakes, and grinding. A withe or stem of a creeper is flattened, heated in the ashes, then drawn tightly round the stone and fastened with string or thongs and gum. With his tomahawk the black cuts his shield, his club, strips bark, constructs his hut, makes his canoe, cuts out the wild honey from the branches of trees, cuts steps up the trees he wants to climb, and many other things too numerous to mention. In short, this instrument he regards as the most valuable by far of which he is possessed.

MESSAGE STICKS.

When a native is sent by his tribe to carry a message to a distant tribe, he always carries a message stick. This is carved and ornamented after a very original fashion. It was at first thought that these carvings were a kind of writing, but later investigation reveals that they are only a confirmation of the messenger's authority and message, which he, as a general rule, delivers first, *viva voce*, and then presents his stick.

They are very often in shape like a miniature boomerang, and colored at both ends with red ochre. All their weapons, with the exception of some kinds of spear, are more or less carved and covered with white and red ochre. The natives have, generally speaking, a considerable taste for carving and drawing. Sheets of bark, on which very good drawings are made, are frequently put up as ornaments in their dwellings.

THE CORROBBOREE.

The corrobboree is a great native dance and theatrical performance combined, in which several tribes take part.

It is usually held when peace is established between tribes which had been previously on bad terms.

It is common to all Australian tribes, although there is great difference in the performances.

It always takes place at night, several fires being kindled to thoroughly light up the scene. The women seat themselves in a body chanting a corrobboree song, while beating most perfect time on their opossum rugs rolled up tight.

Suddenly the dancers make their appearance. Coming out of the gloom of the forest into the bright light, each having his body striped with pipe-clay, so as to resemble, as nearly as possible, a skeleton, with large bunches of green leaves tied tightly about his ankles, which make a peculiar rustling noise as he dances. They become more and more excited, and with loud shouting advance toward their leader, who, chanting the song, retreats backward a little in advance of the dancers till the large fire is reached, when all at the same moment cease dancing and begin stamping with their right feet till a cloud of dust

THE CORROBBOREE.

arises, when with a loud shout they all throw their hands above their heads and the dance ceases, when they retreat to commence again after a little.

One of their corrobboree chants, as given by Mr. Brough Smith, is as follows:

> "Puntin narrinyerar,
> Puntin narrinyerar, O, O, O,
> Yun terpulani ar,
> Tuppim an wangamar,
> Tyiwewar ngoppun ar, O, O, O,
> Puntin narrinyerar," etc.

The above is thus translated:

> "The narinyeri are coming,
> Soon they will appear,
> Carrying kangaroos ;
> Quickly they are coming."

The following is said to be a great favorite as a corrobboree song:

> "Berri berri ma jildomba,
> Berri berri ma jildomba,
> Berri berri ma jildomba-naga,
> Athen jindema no goi-eela,
> Jindema, jindema O-en-dethen-o,
> Warrim bang-e, berri berri ma jildomba-a,
> Berri berri ma jildomba,
> Berri berri ma jildomba."

On some occasions the performance opens with a war dance, when an intricate set of evolutions takes place, accompanied by a brandishing of clubs, spears, boomerangs and shields.

After a few fierce and terrifying yells, they rush together in close fight. Presently one party gives way, and are driven from the field into the dark wood, with roars and groans, and sounds of blows, as well represent a bloody slaughter.

A part of a corrobboree is thus described by one who was present: "A herd of cattle was feeding on the plain, each beast being represented by a native. The imitation was skilful and ludicrously exact.

"Some were lying down, chewing the cud; others stood scratching themselves with hind feet or horns, licking themselves or their calves; several rubbing their heads together.

"Presently a party of blacks was seen creeping towards the cattle, taking all precautions, such as keeping to windward, to prevent the herd from being alarmed. When they got close enough, they speared two head, to the intense delight of the black spectators, who vigorously applauded.

"The hunters next went through the mimic operation of skinning and cutting up and carrying away.

"The next performance was that of a fight between

whites and blacks, the white men being made for the occasion by application of pipe-clay and other paints. The fictitious white men bit the cartridges, put on caps, and went through all the performance of loading and firing. They would wheel to the right, fire, and drive the blacks before them. The latter would rally, and then a desperate fight would follow, when the whites had to give way before the blacks amidst the frantic delight of the spectators.

"When, during the progress of the battle, a black would fall, the spectators would groan, but when a white bit the dust, they would cheer lustily. Thus do these children of nature amuse themselves."

BLACK TRACKERS.

The Governments of the colonies have in their employment blacks whose business it is to track murderers or thieves, or other persons whose apprehension is desired. The scent of the keenest bloodhound could not be more lively than the eyes of these *"trackers."*

Many a poor wretch who has thought himself perfectly safe if he had succeeded in putting a few miles of space between himself and his last night's operations, in a country where snow is not seen, and where, perhaps, much of his walking has been over short, green grass, has been terribly surprised to find himself in the hands of an officer, having been tracked every step of the way. Their cleverness in this respect is the admiration of all the people of Australia.

A sprig or leaf, lately fallen from a tree, pressed more deeply into the grass than it would have been if left wholly to itself; straws pointing in a certain direction; dried thistles, or fern, lately cracked off, and a hundred other things, all taken into account, indicate to these sharp-eyed fellows that their "game" has passed that way.

In some cases these trackers will ride at full gallop over the green and through a village, seeing tracks all the way as easily as we would trace them if they had been made in fresh snow, while to the white man no traces can be seen. Their gift in this respect is very extraordinary.

When any one is lost in the bush the white people rely with the utmost confidence on the "black tracker."

Captain Grey relates how his watch had fallen from his pocket when galloping through the scrub, and over ground of the very worst sort for tracking. "I told 'Kaiber,' my native, of it, and he immediately set out to find it, by retracing our steps. Within a very short time my watch was restored to my pocket."

BLACK TRACKERS. 41

In some parts the blacks themselves, when attacking their enemies by stealth at night, wear a sort of shoe which they call *kooditcha*—invisible spirit. The soles are made of the feathers of the emu, stuck together with human blood, which the maker is said to take from his arm. They are about an inch and a half thick.

The uppers are nets made of human hair. The objects of these shoes is to prevent those who wear them from being tracked and pursued after a night attack. It is only on the softest ground they leave any mark, and even then is impossible to distinguish the heel from the toe.

The blacks say that they can track any thing that walks, except a man shod with *kooditcha*.

One of these fellows, walking over short grass, will tell you at a glance whether a kangaroo or a rabbit has been feeding there during the night. All he may see is the mark on the grass left by the animal's teeth. He knows by the shape of the bite the kind of animal.

In seeking the opossum, which sleeps in hollow trees, during the day, like the raccoon, prowling only at night, he examines the bark, and will tell you at once whether an opossum has lately ascended.

SORCERY AND WITCHCRAFT.

The Australian aborigine is a thorough believer in sorcery, with him it is a great motive power. The principal object to which it is applied is taking the lives of enemies.

They attribute every death of a young or middle-aged person to witchcraft. The first thing necessary is to find out the enemy who has done this. He must be, of course, of another tribe.

The flight of a bird; the direction assumed by a new fallen leaf; the track of a snake or lizard in the fresh ashes strewn about the grave of the departed, or any other trivial circumstance, may indicate to them that the enemy is to be found in the tribe immediately to the east or west of them, as the case may be. An attack is made in the night, and one or more victims of their often ill-directed revenge, will suffice to satisfy them for the loss of their friend.

Sorcery makes them suspect, fear and hate every man not of their own tribe.

As a general rule they are careful to burn all refuse of food, castaway hair or anything else formerly belonging to their persons, lest, if it fall into an enemy's hand he may use it as a means whereby he may hurt them with his sorcery.

All pain is supposed to spring from the same source. The "doctor" sucks the part affected—liver, heart, neck, head or other region of pain—and presently takes from his mouth bits of wood, two inches long, glass or stones, which he has drawn into his mouth from the seat of pain, and which he asserts have been injected into his patient by some hostile doctor. If he fails to effect a cure it is through the more powerful opposing influence of some doctor in a hostile tribe. At least, this excuse quite satisfies the patient or his friends.

When a death occurs the women weep and lament, and tear the skin off their temples with their nails.

The parents of the deceased lacerate themselves fearfully, especially if he be an only son.

The father beats and cuts his head with his tomahawk, and groans bitterly; and the mother sits by the fire and burns her breast and abdomen with a firestick until she wails with pain.

The Rev. George Taplin gives the following account of some of their customs: "The Narranyeri, inhabiting the lakes of the Lower Murray, believe, when a death occurs, that sorcery has caused it.

"The nearest relative sleeps with his head on the corpse, and dreams a dream to discover the name of the sorcerer who has caused the death.

"When the body is being carried to the grave the male members of the tribe gather around it, and keeping their eyes intently upon it, they call out the names of those they think may have practised the sorcery. If it moves when a name is mentioned, then they know on whom to be avenged. As a rule the body does not move (in imagination) until the dreamer mentions the name of the person whom he saw in his dream. The tribe is of course satisfied that the murderer is discovered.

" The bearers immediately begin running as if mad, pretending that the corpse has moved itself, and there are increased signs of deepest mourning. If the supposed one should come to the lamentation the dreamer watches him closely, and if he does not shed tears he is the more convinced of his guilt, and considers it now his duty to avenge his relative's death. If the suspected one should happen to be of their own nation a difficulty arises.

"They may not desire to kill the sorcerer. Negotiations result in the injured family or tribe formally cursing the slayer of their friend and all his relations. If this is done arrangements are at once made for a fight. The mourning tribe commence to weep and lament as soon as they see their foes. The latter mock and deride them, and some of them dance wild dances, flourishing their spears. They shout and laugh wildly, and do all in their power to provoke a fight. If there is any old grudge between the two tribes they fight savagely, and sometimes two or three may be killed; but if they are met merely to '*give satisfaction*' for the injury done to the dead man, the fight is interrupted after a few spears are thrown by some old man, who declares that enough has been done. If the old men on both sides agree, the hostile tribes again mingle on friendly terms, and there is an end of the business, for the death has been avenged."

There are three forms of sorcery, says Mr. Curr, called "millin," "ngathungi," and "neilyeri."

Millin.—A big-headed club called "plongge" is used entirely for millin. A mere touch from it is the cause of disease and death. They sometimes knock down an enemy, then tap his chest with the plongge, hit him with it on his shoulders and knees, and pull his ears till they crack. He is then called *plongge wategeri*. He is now, by this means, given to the power of a demon called Nalkaru, who will create disease in his chest, or cause him to be speared in battle or bitten by a snake. Very frequently the plongge is used upon a person sleeping. It is warmed, and the chest of the sleeper is gently tapped. Such an one is sure to have, as they think, disease of the chest. If any one feels sore in the chest after sleeping, it is always attributed to the touch of the plongge.

Ngathungi.—This form of sorcery is practised with bones, or remains of animals which have been eaten. A bone of some bird or beast which an enemy has eaten is obtained. This is mixed with grease, red-ochre and human hair. The mass is stuck in a round lump on the end of a skewer of kangaroo's bone, and is then called "ngathungi." When injury is intended against the man who ate the animal from which the bone came, the ball above described is put down before the fire, and as it melts disease is supposed to be engendered in the person so bewitched, and if it wholly melts he dies. Any one who knows that another person has ngathungi capable of injuring him, buys it if he can and throws it in the river or lake. This breaks the charm.

Neilyeri.—This is practised by means of a pointed bone. It is scraped to a very fine point. Sometimes an iron point is used. This is poisoned by being stuck into a dead body. Any one wounded by it usually loses a limb or dies. Sometimes this wound is inflicted secretly, when the person is asleep. The bone is kept moist by being wrapped in human hair soaked in liquor from a dead body. The natives are so terribly afraid of neilyeri that they dread even to have the weapon pointed at them, looking upon it as having a deadly energy, even when thus used.

SPIRITS—GOOD AND BAD.

All the tribes seemed to be thoroughly convinced of the existence of evil spirits. Of course, each will have its own name for the chief of these demons. Otherwise there is not much difference.

The Dieyerie tribe call the Evil One "*Kootchie.*" Nearly every case of sickness or death arising from apparently natural causes, is ascribed to *Kootchie.*

When it thunders, it is *Kootchie growling.* If it thunders long and loud, the whole tribe will rush out, and, elevating their hands, they will cry out simultaneously, "*Hoo! Hoo!*" to frighten Kootchie away.

If wild pigeons coo in the night, they are very much frightened and excited, for they are sure it is the Evil Spirit which occasions it.

Whirlwinds come, as they think, from the same source. Should a whirlwind approach the camp, they throw boomerangs at it.

With some tribes this spirit is known as *Muuruup* (mooroop). He visits the earth in lightning. He it is who knocks down trees. He is hated and feared. Owls are his agents. When an owl hoots, the children creep under their rugs. He is not feared much in daylight, but greatly dreaded at night.

If children are troublesome, they are quieted with "Ka-ka-mooroop" (come here, devil). I used to be told when I was little, and bad, of course, that the "old *black* man" would get me. Little did I then think that he would turn out to be an Australian native.

Mooroop lives under ground, where there is nothing but fire, and where bad people get no meat nor drink, but where they are terribly knocked about by the evil spirits.

Throughout Victoria this being is known as *Bunyip*. He is very voracious in his appetite for human beings. Its groanings and bellowings can be heard by all natives living near swamps or lagoons. One day a woman fishing in a pond for eels, caught them as fast as her husband could carry them to the camp.

It turned out to be just as the husband feared, a trick on the part of the Bunyip thus to entice the woman to come and fish when her husband was not present, and so one day Bunyip swallowed her (as was supposed), for her husband never could find her. In the Western Port region the Bunyip is known as *Tooroo-dun*.

Some writers think that these people have no knowledge of God whatever, and have no forms of native

SPIRITS—GOOD AND BAD.

worship. It seems to be true respecting some of the tribes, but not so of all.

By the word *Nooralie*, one writer (Mr. Bulmer) says the blacks understand a Superior Being, who has existed for ages and ages, and still exists. Of the belief of the Cape River tribes another writer says: "When a black fellow dies, whose actions have been what they regard as good, he is said to ascend to *Boorala* (*i.e.*, to the Creator, literally *Good*). The milky way is said to be the smoke from celestial grass, set fire to by departed women, as a signal to direct the dead to the eternal camp fires of the tribe."

As we have sometimes represented to our children the chief of demons as the "old black man," so, without intending it, however, as a retaliation, some of the tribes speak of the devil as a "*white* man." And with very good reason, I think, if we consider the barbarities of some of the early squatters; and the wickedness of some of these men even at this day can hardly be surpassed by any heathen or pagan.

Among some of the tribes there seems to have been an idea of the return of the spirit of man to the earth again, but, if so, he was to return white. "In early times," says Curr, "white men, seen by blacks, were thought to be their deceased countrymen come back to them." To some of these they gave names such as had belonged to their more distinguished ancestors.

In some of their vocabularies, *white men* and *ghosts* are expressed by the same term.

CREATION AND THE DELUGE.

The tribes in the Gippsland country (a part of the colony of Victoria) believe that the Creator of all that has life upon earth was a gigantic black fellow who lived in Gippsland many centuries ago, and now dwells among the stars. Many of the stars are named after some of their people long since dead. *Venus* is called *noorut*, which means *wombat* hunter. These tribes have also a tradition of the deluge which runs somewhat as follows:

Long ages ago there was no water at all in what are now the lakes, rivers and seas known to them or their fathers, for an immense frog had swallowed up the whole of it.

All the animals and fishes held a consultation, and came to the conclusion that the only remedy was to make the frog laugh, and then there would be plenty of water.

To this end every animal came before the frog in the most ridiculous postures imaginable, and went through the funniest antics. For a long time they failed, until the eel stood upon the tip of his tail, and wriggled about so comically that the big frog literally burst with laughter, and the water poured from him in such vast streams that there was presently a deluge, and all the blacks would have been drowned had not one of them made a large canoe by which some of them were saved.

KINDNESS OF HEART.

Though there is a great deal of cruelty among the natives, much of it is the result of their superstition, yet occasionally there are evidences of real kind-heartedness. As an instance of this we have the following:—It is a law among them that when one has been convicted of stealing, he is punished by being struck a terrible blow over the head, the person from whom the theft has been made being usually the executioner.

One had stolen some sugar from another of his tribe. He was sentenced to receive the ordinary punishment. The man who had been wronged struck a blow which would have smashed the skull of a white man. The other never stirred, but simply looked up, the blood streaming down his face. The executioner looked him in the face, then turned the weapon on himself, and with two or three blows, sent the blood streaming down his own face, then casting away the weapon, threw his arms around the neck of the culprit and sobbed like a child.

A story is told of a war between one of the tribes and some of the natives of New Zealand. The Australians being put to rout, fled across a river in such haste that a little child was left behind. The New Zealander held up the child, when the father, though conscious that he was running a great risk, yet impelled by parental love, waded across the stream for it, but as he came close up to the shore to receive it, he was brained by the tomahawk of the treacherous *Maori*, and both he and his child floated down the river together.

When death enters the family, the relatives exhibit the most intense grief. They cover their heads with clay and daub their faces with the same material. If a man dies his wives cut and burn themselves in a most shocking manner, and their wail is most melancholy and heartrending. As a general rule mothers show much affection for their children, and are, therefore, not permitted to see, or even come near, when the cruel ceremonies of initiation into manhood are performed upon the young men. Even the old men themselves sometimes weep over these cruelties.

What may seem to us as evidence of great cruelty

in their vengeance on other tribes is in them nothing more or less than the outcome of their ideas of justice. Their superstition leads them to fix upon certain persons as guilty of destroying their innocent friends, and justice demands that they should avenge the wrong. The voice of their brother's blood cries unto them, as Abel's did to heaven, and they dare not turn a deaf ear.

THE CRUELTIES OF PAGANISM.

Jesus Christ has said, "Take My yoke upon you."

Did you ever think that His yoke is heavy and in any sense "grievous to be borne?" Of all the yokes which men must bear His yoke is the easiest and lightest of all.

The cruelties of paganism it is not possible to describe.

Some may have thought that these innocent children of nature are as happy as we can make them if we go to them with the Gospel.

"Leave them alone," they say. You will only disturb them if you intrude upon them new ideas. They are more happy as they are.

Those who thus write and speak know little of the social condition of the pagan.

If we look very briefly at the condition of the

Australian native, we shall see this verified. The male, as is mentioned elsewhere in this book, must submit to have one or more of his teeth knocked out, to have the cartilage of his nose pierced, to have most painful cuttings and scarifyings in his skin.

The youth, in the majority of cases, is seized when about eighteen years of age, and forced to submit to two especially terrible mutilations, which cannot be described here. Besides, he is positively prohibited from using a large number of the most tempting kinds of meats and fruits throughout more than half of his natural life.

In this respect superstition alone is his motive power.

From his infancy he has been taught that violation of these rules, which his fathers have observed from time immemorial, will be sure to be followed by disease, calamity or death. So firmly fixed is this thought in the minds of young men, that when hunting with white men, they could not possibly be induced to partake of the meat of the emu, or certain portions of other birds and animals.

From his earliest recollections the poor pagan boy has listened to the wonders and horrors of sorcery, and he constantly trembles lest some of these things should befall him.

The hooting of an owl, the voice of the thunder, the very cooing of the pigeons in the night, are to him sources of fear and alarm.

The yoke of sorcery, witchcraft, and superstition continually galls him.

If that of the male is heavy, the yoke of the female is still more grievous. She has also to submit to physical mutilation; in some tribes one joint of the forefinger, in others, two joints of the little finger. In some tribes also she is scarified in various parts of the body, somewhat as the young men are. Some kinds of food are denied her also.

As regards her marriage, she has, as a general rule, no choice. She is the *property* of her father or his heirs until married, after that the *property* of her husband.

In many cases she has to submit to become the wife of a man whom she hates and dreads. If she offers anything like a stubborn resistance, a few blows over the head from a club in her father's hand usually results in a quiet submission on her part.

They are in most cases married at fourteen, some even younger, and are usually mothers at fifteen or sixteen.

If the father thinks the child ought not to live she must strangle it at his command.

In some cases, where death may have resulted from

natural causes, but of course believed to have been caused by sorcery from another tribe, the mother is forced to carry about the dead body for weeks, laying her head upon it at night, if, peradventure, she may there dream who has caused the child's death. Instances are on record where the mother herself has died as the result of this horrible custom.

"Wives have to undergo all the drudgery of the camp and the march, having the poorest food, and the hardest work, and are occasionally cruelly beaten or speared for even the most trifling offence."—*Curr*.

So that, although they are not altogether without some joyful days, having at times some sources of amusement, yet their lot in the main is a hard one, and their yoke a heavy one.

In common with her male relations she has to suffer all those terrors which are the natural fruit of their systems of sorcery and superstition. Tribes live in constant dread of each other. Witchcraft is liable to charge almost any one at any time with having caused the death of some one of another tribe.

Immediately the avenger of blood is on his track, he may receive a blow from behind his back at a moment when he is least suspecting, and so he is more or less always suspecting it.

Or the avenger may surprise him in his sleep or in the early dawn, he knows not when.

The outcome of all this is, every man of any tribe looks upon all men of other tribes as their natural enemies, and so must necessarily hate all men save those with whom they are each day associated. Such is the yoke of paganism.

EXTINCTION OF THE RACE.

The Australian settlers have not dealt as kindly with the natives as they should have done.

From the beginning the white man has thoroughly ignored any right or title to the land on the part of the aborigines.

Squatters taking up large runs for sheep and cattle, must have been perfectly well aware that they were usurping territory which had been the undisturbed possession of other men for centuries.

The natives found the animals upon which they and their fathers had depended for ages for food, driven out by the white man.

They dare not encroach upon the territory of a neighboring tribe for game or food of any sort without violating those sacred regulations which had always controlled the tribes in their amicable relations to each other.

To have thus transgressed their own native laws would necessarily have resulted in tribal wars.

A tribe finding itself hemmed in and pressed for food would not consent, on the one hand, to wrong their native neighbors, nor, on the other, to starve while food was so near at hand, as that which now occupied the former grazing grounds of the kangaroo and the emu, so they did that which any one of us would expect them to do, they speared the squatter's sheep and cattle.

At once war was declared on the part of the squatter. He and his men made no conscience of shooting down the blacks as they would shoot down a dingo. Resistance with clubs and spears was of small account when it arrayed itself against the rifle.

Sometimes the Government stepped in to aid the squatter in his work of usurpation of the rightful property of others, and his extinction of the possessors. Native mounted police were employed under the control and direction of a white "inspector."

There was no difficulty in getting these men to do their unnatural work most effectually, if only removed 200 or 300 miles away from their own tribe, and, of course, nearly as far from any tribe whom they had formerly known.

These fellows, set on by their "inspector," and thoroughly trained by him in the use of the rifle and revolver, were as eager for their work as bloodhounds.

The men of the offending tribe were shot down by the score, and the women were handed over by the *worthy* official to his "boys" for a fate worse than that which had befallen their husbands, their sons, and their brothers. When the bloody and wicked campaign, which could not last very long, was over, the inspector simply reported that the tribe had been "dispersed."

What the rifle failed to do, *intoxicants* and diseases, some of them of the most loathsome kind, all unknown previously to the blacks, have done—destroyed these poor creatures by thousands. With these destructive forces at work for the last half century or more, the native population has been in all the settled portions of Victoria, New South Wales, and South Australia, largely swept off. With the mere fraction which remains, the Government and people of the present day are dealing more kindly. A part of the remnant are gathered upon "reservations." They have schools and churches, and domestic comforts, of which their fathers knew not.

All this, however, does not atone for the wicked treatment which has been shown multitudes of their race, by a people who should have had more honor and humanity.

Little good can come, perhaps, from berating those on whom now devolve the responsibilities of government for the sins committed by those who went before them.

Let those, however, who feel an interest in the honor and fair fame of their country (and Australians have many things of which they may justly be proud), put forth a greater effort to educate and save the remnant of these native people. Some of them may be very low, and offer little encouragement for effort, but others are brighter, especially among the children, as I can testify from personal observation in some of the schools I visited. I hold that they all have a just claim upon the humane and philanthropic efforts of the stronger race which has displaced them.

AUSTRALIAN NATIVE'S NECKLACE.

THE AUSTRALIAN ANIMALS.

THEY have in Australia nearly one hundred and sixty varieties of mammalian animals, and yet they have among them, as native, no horses, oxen, sheep, goats, antelopes, apes, elephants, wolves, bears, pigs, hares, rabbits, or squirrels. In their stead they have kangaroo, dingoes, sloths, bandicot, wombat, flying fox, flying opossum, and a variety of climbing opossum, and the native cat.

Nearly all of these are marsupial. This is a characteristic of Australian animals, and is unknown, or nearly so, in all other parts of the world.

THE KANGAROO.

There are not less than forty different species of kangaroo. This number includes, of course, those which are generally called *wallabies*. There are the great kangaroo, which is, when full grown, of about two hundred pounds weight. The sooty kangaroo, western kangaroo, red kangaroo, rock kangaroo, brush kangaroo, and nail-tailed kangaroo. The hare kangaroo, very fleet, six kinds. The bettong or jerboa kangaroo, weighing from three to six pounds; they climb very readily; there are several species. Kangaroo rats, several species. There are also red wallaroo and black wallaroo, Parry's wallaby, black wallaby, red-necked wallaby, black-striped wallaby and black-gloved wallaby; pademelons, six kinds.

The wallaby is usually a darker color and coarser-haired animal than the kangaroo proper. These all belong, however, to the same class in the animal kingdom.

Some of the kangaroos, when standing upright, as they usually do if danger is suspected near them, are quite six feet or more in height. We went into the forest one day kangaroo hunting. The first one I saw was standing up; unfortunately my piece was loaded with shot, for which he was too far off. I succeeded, however, in starting the "mob," which crossed the forest towards the points where the dogs and horsemen were placed. The dogs soon took the scent, and in a short time we had a good two-year-old specimen for our game.

I aided in skinning the animal, and in doing so was thoroughly convinced that the theory of their using their tail as a lever or propelling force is quite incorrect. I found men in Australia who have lived there for over a quarter of a century who fully believe this theory The tail serves as a balance, nothing more. Not only

THE KANGAROO.

is there no callosity at all on the under side of the tail, but there is finer fur.

If the tail were used, as some writers have told us, there would not only be no hair, but it would be very much calloused. In neither case is this so.

We walked a mile next morning to see a tame one. I particularly watched his locomotion, and my notions respecting the matter were fully confirmed—the tail is merely a balance.

They are very easily tamed, and when tamed are very affectionate. They can be taught quite as easily as one can teach a dog.

Give him his tin cup and tell him to go for milk, and he will take the cup in his fore-paws and leap away for it quite as fast as a boy will run.

They feed upon grass, and for this reason they are hunted and destroyed by the sheep and cattle owners. This enmity towards them, on the part of the graziers, will end by-and-bye in their complete destruction. They are rapidly disappearing from all the older settlements.

They are marsupials, *i.e.*, they carry their young in a pouch.

We saw in the Zoological Gardens at Melbourne a white female kangaroo feeding quite near us; and as we stood looking at her a young one, about the size of a full-grown cat, put its head out of the pouch and began nibbling the grass too. To those who have never seen such a thing before, it is not only most interesting as a novel development of animal life, but highly amusing.

When hotly pursued by the dogs the mother will sometimes throw the young one from the pouch, by which the dogs are checked, and she makes her escape.

One cannot help feeling, if he loses sight for a moment of the existence of a great all-wise Creator, who does many things we cannot understand, that in the production of the kangaroo, some way nature has made a mistake.

In looking at them moving along, with their *hop, skip* and *jump* locomotion, there is excited for them the deepest sympathy, for your first impression is that they are naturally deformed, and in giving them chase you are simply trying to destroy a cripple which cannot give any hunter a very exalted opinion of himself.

However, this is judgment formed on first appearance only. Give him chase, as a general rule he will take as good care of himself as any other game. I am told these animals have been known to jump, when closely pursued, thirty feet of a clear jump.

When they are overtaken, and find themselves un-

THE KANGAROO. 65

able to keep up the pace, instinct guides them to turn with their back to a tree. When attacked in front, there is considerable danger for either dog or man, from the terrible spike on the middle toe of the hind foot. .

One well-directed stroke from either hind foot will often render *hors de combat* the attacking force.

A well-aimed blow from a scimitar could not be worse.

If very closely pressed in front they sometimes seize their enemy in the same way as the bears are said to do, with a *loving* (?) embrace. Then with a blow or two from the spike, that hug becomes very frequently to the enemy the *hug* of death.

In one instance an "*old man kangaroo*" took to the water. The dog followed him. He seized the dog in his fore-paws and thrust him under the water and drowned him. The owner of the dog rushed in to save him, but the "old man" laid hold of him also, and threw him down and would certainly have drowned him, too, if his companion had not come to his assistance.

"Are they good to eat?" Well—that all depends. If you are very hungry and cannot get any other animal food, you may relish one meal. It is good for the natives, so we will leave it to them to enjoy.

The tail, however, is largely used and very much relished for soup.

It is, I think, as good as ox-tail, from which it cannot very easily be distinguished if well spiced.

One very great objection to kangaroo meat, from whatever part of the body it may be taken, is its marked lack of juiciness. In this particular, however, it does not differ from several other kinds of wild meat.

Wild game of any kind in Australia for the table does not bear favorable comparison with that of Canada. This may be accounted for partly, so far as birds are concerned, by the almost entire absence of those wild berries and fruits, which Canada produces in such profuse abundance, and both this and that may be largely explained by the sad lack of those refreshing and life-giving rains with which a benign Providence has so kindly favored our northern land.

For nearly one-half the year (occasionally more than one-half) the fields and forests of Australia are literally parched. What the sun may not do, in the way of withering the grass, the hot winds from the north, coming down over the country as out of a blast furnace, take the greenness, and almost the life, out of vegetation, so that, upon the whole, animal life in its native condition is not so favored nor so flourishing as with us.

THE DINGO.

Among the native animals of Australia is the dingo, or native dog.

One can hardly bring himself to believe, when look-

THE DINGO, OR NATIVE AUSTRALIAN DOG.

ing at them in the zoological gardens, or as they appear in the picture, that they are wild animals.

They are, however, of so wild a nature that it is very rarely they can be domesticated.

The blacks, by getting them when they are only a few days old, can sometimes succeed.

As a general rule, even they fail. When others have tried, they have found that the wild nature will prevail in time over the most careful domestication, and the dingo will return to the forest and to the native habits of his kind.

Those we saw were in the Zoological Gardens of Melbourne and Adelaide, and were just as handsome and as innocent looking as those you see here in the picture.

A fox always looks as if there was something wrong with his conscience; the wolf, as if he has no conscience, and does not desire any, for it might be terribly in his way. The dingo looks as if he does not need one, he is so innocent, so perfectly pure in all his intentions, so affectionate. Look at him, and see if this is not his character, so far as his countenance is concerned, and yet, for a downright hypocritical scoundrel, he is by far the first of the three. He is more cunning than the fox. His depredations upon the sheep and poultry of the Australian farmer are so great that a bounty of thirty shillings (about $7) per scalp is offered by the Governments of some of the colonies.

One or two of them have been known to kill as many as forty sheep in a night.

They seem to worry the sheep for the mere pleasure it gives them, for it is very seldom they eat any of the animal after they have killed it. They are so cunning that it is almost useless to set traps for them.

Their sense of smell is so acute that persons who put out poisoned meat for them are obliged to handle the meat with a fork in preparing and placing it, as they will not touch it if it has on it the smell of a human hand, and in this you cannot deceive them, especially in those districts where the white man has proved himself to be their enemy.

He does not bark. His cry is precisely that of the jackal. Some maintain that the dingo and the jackal are one species; however, that is disputed.

It is argued by some persons that he is not a native of Australia, because not a marsupial, as about all of the fur-bearing animals of Australia are. Those familiar with the natural history of the island-continent put them down as native, and so, for the present, at any rate, they must be regarded.

Sir Thomas Mitchell, speaking of the doings and efforts of the natives to tame the brute, says that the native women are often seen nursing them as they nurse their children, and it is not an uncommon occurrence to see a woman with a child at one breast and a young dog at the other.

This kindness towards those they attempt to domesticate does not prevent them from slaughtering the wild dingo whenever and wherever they can.

When they catch one by trapping he is killed and thrown on the fire and singed. Then he is drawn and afterward roasted in an oven constructed of heated stones. The carcass is covered with bark or grass and earth. In the course of two hours or more he is well cooked and fit to be eaten.

Mr. Curr says, "The Australian dingo is not wanting in courage. When pinned in a corner he will attack a man, and exhibit all the fierceness of a watchdog. He is not unlike the sheep-dog, but he resembles also the fox, and when enraged has a wolf-like aspect. A full-grown, fairly well-fed dingo is about two feet in height, and two feet six inches in length. His head is like that of the fox, his ears are erect, but not long. His color varies from a yellowish tawny to a reddish brown, growing lighter towards the belly, and the tip of his brush is generally white. He has a habit of turning his head over his shoulder when he looks at a supposed enemy, something like the fox."

Returning for a little to the claim of the dingo to be counted a genuine native of Australia, in sinking for water near Tower Hill, in the western part of Victoria, bones and skulls of dingoes were found not only very many feet below the surface, but below blue and yellow clay. And at Lake Timboon the bones of the wild dog were found with those of the Tasmanian devil (*sarcophilus ursinus*), now extinct on the main land, and only found living in Tasmania.

It is now beyond doubt that the dingo was once co-temporaneous with the now extinct marsupial lion, which in former ages roamed through the forests of Australia.

I was told an amusing story in which a dingo figured, and I give it to my reader that he may also have the benefit of it.

There was an enthusiastic reader of the Bible living in one of the towns of New South Wales, who maintained that nothing ever occurred to us in our daily experience which could not be represented or illustrated by some passage in the Bible. His friends used to chaff him on it, but he could not be shaken.

One day he came some little distance for the purpose of bathing in the sea, and he brought with him a luncheon of sandwich, which he wrapped (to prevent its drying with the hot sun) inside his coat and shirt, laying the parcel down upon the beach, and then went a few rods further down, and removing his pantaloons, went in. While he was swimming about a dingo came down from the scrub on the hill, and smelling the dinner, snatched the parcel and made off with it. When the man came out of the water he had no clothes left but the covering for his lower extremities. He called loudly, till at last some one came to his assistance.

When he told of the affair to some of his friends, they said, "Now, John, you could not find any Scripture for such an experience as that."

"Oh," he said, "I think there must be."

He was answered that it was quite impossible; there could not be anything in the Bible that was anything like that. "Well," said he, "let me think a little—O, I have it—'And Asher continued on the sea shore, and abode in his breaches' (breeches)."— *Song of Deborah, in the Book of Judges.*

SULPHUR-CRESTED COCKATOO.

THE AUSTRALIAN BIRDS.

THERE are about seven hundred species of birds in Australia. Of these, a goodly number resemble birds known almost everywhere. Hawks, eagles, owls, cranes, crows, swallows, though differing somewhat from birds of that name in other countries, yet there is considerably more similarity than difference.

Of the owls there are the *masked*, the *sooty*, the *delicate*, *rufous*, *winking*, and the "*Boobook*." This last is a native name, given it in imitation of the cry of the bird.

There are no song-birds. These are not numerous as distinct species in any country. In the wide continent of America, when you have named the robin, thrush, cat-bird, and lark, you have pretty nearly exhausted the list, though there are many which utter a very pleasant note or two.

In Australia there are none which can be counted song-birds. The myna-bird begins very like the robin and gives you about three notes, then he stops and begins again.

I have often experienced a real sense of disappointment in listening to these birds.

What Australian birds lack in song, however, they make up in plumage.

Go where you will, by rail or coach, you cannot fail, a little distance from the cities, to see some of these bright plumaged birds, and we had in this respect a fine opportunity. We travelled thousands of miles through the country parts in passing from one town or village to another.

Besides, specimens of almost all the bright plumed birds are in the zoological gardens, so that where one fails to see them in their native wilds, he can see them in the cages.

I have found that the very best source of information respecting birds, especially of this kind, is the enthusiastic taxidermist, who every now and then spends several days in the forest, procuring birds and rare animals for himself.

THE COCKATOO.

There are, it is said, not less than sixty different kinds of parrots; some authors say seventy. I presume the cockatoos are reckoned among these.

The white cockatoo, with the large yellow crest, is the most common of the cockatoo variety. I have seen these in hundreds feeding in the fields. They are as great a pest to the farmer as the crow of America.

They are a very wise bird as regards their precautions for self-protection

They never descend from the forest to feed in the fields without placing sentinels at every principal

ROSE HILL PARRAKEETS.

point of the compass, to give timely warning of any approaching danger. It is almost impossible to get within gunshot of them

They are, as a general rule, secured for market by the natives or others visiting the nests at the proper season, and bringing away the young. They are capital speakers. Very amusing stories are told of some of them in this respect.

A young man was trying to get near a flock for a shot. They were very shy, and kept moving on and on, just keeping out of range. One seemed more bold and careless than the rest, so he thought he would give attention to that one, and using a good deal of caution he at last got close enough and raised his gun to shoot, when the bird said, "Won't grandmother give it to you when you get home?" He lowered his gun and walked straight away, having no more heart in him for shooting cockatoos. The bird had doubtless escaped after a year or two of domestication. We saw many of them in the large cages at the public gardens, some of them speaking very distinctly. The most common expression we heard from them was, "Cocky wants a bit of bread." No child could say this any better.

The most beautiful of the cockatoo species is the corella, or, as he is called by some, "Leadbeater's cockatoo." This is also white with pink-tipped wings, but is smaller than the yellow-crested. Its crest is mottled pink and white. When standing at ease, the crest is laid back upon the neck so closely that at a little distance you would scarcely notice it. The

LEADBEATER'S COCKATOO.

moment something near in front startles it (as extending your hand towards it quickly), the changed appearance of the bird, together with its increased beauty, is most extraordinary.

If you will raise your eight fingers in a perpendicular line, immediately in front of you, and suddenly throw them forward, spreading them slightly apart as you do so, you will get some idea of the action of this most beautiful speaking-bird of Australia, when quickly startled or when he is on speaking terms with you.

A countryman came into the train with me, with a young one in a cage. He said he had taken it from the nest only a few days before, and I could see it was but a chicken, for it was only partly feathered, yet the feathers of the crest were quite two and a half inches in length and most beautifully marked.

We brought with us a stuffed specimen, as we could not so conveniently bring a live one.

Then there are the black, the gray, the red-breasted, and the "gang-gang" cockatoo, besides the cockatoo-parrot, which the natives call *kooranyawillawilla*.

THE PARROT.

Among the parrots are the rosehill, white, red, crimson, king, green-leck, king-lory blue mountain,

ROSELLA PARROT.

Pennant's parrot, grass parrot, ground parrakeet, and the rosella. This last-named is the commonest of all. It is to be seen everywhere—sometimes in flocks in

THE PARROT.

the orchards and pasture grounds, sometimes in pairs in the yards about the houses. In almost every house you find at least one in a cage, ready to chatter and whistle to everybody who will notice him.

As it was not possible (or at any rate convenient) to

A TALKER.

bring so far any living specimens, we brought instead a goodly number of stuffed ones.

There are other birds than parrots in Australia that can be taught to speak—such as the myna-bird, the lyre-bird, the honey-bird (a cut of which is given), the laughing-jackass or giant kingfisher, and the Australian magpie, which can speak very distinctly. Wife and I were walking through the market, and stepped up to mag's cage, when she said in good, plain English: "Who are you?" "Oh," I said, "Mag, I'm afraid you don't attend temperance meetings, though I have no doubt you are a sensible, cold-water bird." The Australian magpie has not that thieving, mischievous propensity which characterizes his English cousin. They are not only a harmless bird, but very useful as grub-destroyers. There is a law against killing them. They are to be seen almost everywhere, sometimes in great numbers. They have no song. They have, however, a very metallic, musical note which is varied with a full, round whistle. This metallic note has secured for them from some ornithologists the name of "bellbird," though they are never recognized by that name in Australia.

The only representation I can give of a magpie chorus in the early morning is that of fifty boys, half of whom are tapping with small hammers upon anvils, while the others are sounding short notes at the same time on fifes and flutes.

WAVED PARROT.

THE LYRE-BIRD.

The lyre-bird is, I presume, the shyest bird known. I am told that it is impossible to tame it. Its resort is just as far from civilization as possible. Only the natives can claim to have much knowledge of them. The hunter has to use the greatest caution to get within reach of them.

Those white men who have camped in the wilderness, or the early settlers who have heard them in the scrub some distance away, tell us that they have the power to imitate almost any sound which may arrest their attention, such as the barking of a dog, the loud snapping of a whip, the *cooéé* of the bushman or the herder, or the ring of the axe upon the hard trees.

The lyre-bird has no beauty whatever except in his tail. For this there is considerable demand. It is sometimes difficult to get them. We were able, however, to procure a pair, which we very highly prize.

THE KINGFISHER.

There is a large variety of kingfishers throughout the continent. Besides the species especially mentioned below, there are the following: Leach's kingfisher, fawn-breasted kingfisher, sacred kingfisher, red-backed kingfisher, sordid kingfisher, MacLeay's kingfisher, yellow-billed kingfisher, white-tailed kingfisher, azure kingfisher, little kingfisher.

I procured three specimens. One of these is about the size of a swallow, with two tail-feathers about six inches long, very prettily marked.

The most widely-known, and at the same time the most popular, bird in Australia, is the laughing jackass, or *giant kingfisher*. He is by no means a timid bird. There is a heavy penalty for any one killing him, and he not only seems to know that there is such a law, but he has apparently perfect confidence in the law which protects him, so why should he not laugh when he wants to? and he will come right up to your door, or perch upon the plum tree or the barn, and laugh till he makes you laugh a response, unless there is something wrong with your liver.

Though he is, properly speaking, a *kingfisher*, he makes it his special business to fish for snakes. What he does not know about catching snakes we shall not try to teach him. Perhaps it is just after he has had a square meal from an old copper-head or one of his cousins, that he has his best laugh.

Turning to our picture for a moment, I should think the two in the rear have just finished a jolly dinner of snake, but have failed to extend an invitation to the poor, disconsolate-looking old fellow in

LAUGHING JACKASS.

front. He does look sad, now, does he not? All the more so while he is forced to listen to the uproarious fun of his two neighbors immediately behind him. Never mind, "Jack," you will have your turn presently. "He laughs best who laughs last."

You evidently feel slighted and hurt, we all know what that means. Laughing men and laughing jackasses have a common experience in some respects. Do you know, reader, the first prerequisite for a good dinner of snake? Get your snake. That is what our friend who is foremost in the picture is probably now looking for. He is not going to wait long.

There are many kinds of snakes, and several of them are venomous. That is why these birds are so carefully protected.

If his snakeship should happen to be a good sized one and a little refractory, the bird will ascend very rapidly directly over rocks or over the hard road, to the height of three or four hundred feet, and let him fall. If the snake should seem to be a little too lively after his fall, he gets a second one inside of a minute, after which he is perfectly manageable.

Like every good laugher he does best when he has plenty of company, and really one of the most amusing things you will hear in Australia is a laughing chorus from three or four, or more, of these very queer birds.

One begins with long drawn a-h, then the others strike in. It is quite easy to distinguish the different voices, "hah-hah," "hah-hah," mingled with "haw-haw-haw," "hoh-hoh-hoh," in rapid succession, then a lull followed by another outburst, till the forest rings again with their merry peals.

"Is it a laugh?" Well, now, please don't ask too many questions. I don't know.

You remember the story of the colored brother who was expatiating on the creation of man, and said, "When de Lawd made Adam outen de clay, He stood him up agin de fence to dry." "Hold on dah, brudder," said a sable hearer, "how'd dat fence come dah so nice and handy?" "Will you please to shut up?" responded the preacher; "a few questions like dat'd spile de best theology in de wuld."

I do not know whether the noise of the laughing jackass is the outcome of merriment or not. It may be that under any form of excitement he would make the same sound. I have had very good opportunity for observing them in the cage, in the forest, and in the yards about residences, and, as far as my observation goes, the bird only makes this noise when he is in a pleasant mood, so I suppose we may regard his laugh as not only strongly resembling that of our own race, but as also meaning about the same thing.

THE BOWER-BIRD.

Among the strange habited birds of Australia is the bower-bird.

This bird gets its name from the fact that it builds a bower for, as it would seem, a kind of play-house.

BOWER-BIRDS.

I have seen this bower, and bird. It is a little larger than the American robin—a light brown, slightly speckled with spots of darker brown.

Choosing, say, a little spot of grass, a patch in the plain, it beats down a pathway, or perhaps, if necessary, removes the grass for a pathway, about four inches wide, and from two to three feet in length. Over this it weaves together the top of the grass from both sides, and then, from far and near, it brings small bones which it finds bleached white on the plains, bits of colored glass, pieces of red flannel, if it can find them anywhere.

With the bones, colored glass, bright pebbles, and other things of that kind it will pave the pathway through the bower, while the red flannel, bits of tin, or bright feathers which have fallen from some of the prettier birds, it will weave into the grass above the bower.

Naturalists were puzzled for some time respecting the bird's object, but all are now satisfied, I think, that the only object is to afford pleasure for himself and his companions. They have been seen chasing each other through and through the bower, apparently thoroughly enjoying their fun.

THE BRUSH-TURKEY.

The habits of the brush-turkey are quite as interesting as those of any I have described. Several of these birds will join together in building up a mound of grass or vegetable matter of any kind, in which they will—perhaps a half dozen of them—deposit their eggs, and allow them to be hatched out by the heat engendered by decomposition. Each successive year they merely add to the heap enough fresh matter to answer the purpose of hatching a new setting. This is a more extraordinary instinct than that of the ostrich which deposits her eggs in the hot sand.

THE REGENT-BIRD.

To return for a little to the bright plumaged birds, we see the wonderful provision which the great Creator has made to prevent their extinction. Take for illustration that wonderfully beautiful specimen the *regent-bird*.

That man may not be tempted to destroy the female she is a very plain gray bird. There is very little attraction for the eye in looking at her. The male bird of one year old is just as plain as the female. The only way by which he can be known from the female, is that about one-half his beak has turned a light yellow. Of course this cannot be seen by the sportsman or bright plumage seeker, and he sees no reason why he should shoot him. At two years old the male bird has changed somewhat, but not much. There are some yellow spots on his wings. At three years he has changed a good deal more, but it is not until his fourth year that he reaches his great beauty.

For two full years he has been pairing and reproducing his species, through all this time quite safe, because he has no attractive beauty.

An enthusiastic taxidermist in Melbourne had in a case, stuffed, the five specimens, the female and one male of each year up to the fourth, and through him we learned many most interesting facts respecting the *regent*, and other birds and animals of Australia.

To me, however, that new world presented such a variety of interesting subjects, that I found great pleasure in observing for myself, and then asking many questions of those who seemed to have quite as much pleasure in answering them, besides reading every book I could find bearing on these subjects, though I had no intention at the time of making a book.

THE EMU.

The emu, or *New Holland cassowary* ought, I suppose, to be classed with the ostrich, which it resembles. It stands five or six feet high. Its feathers are more like coarse hair than like feathers. Its flesh is like coarse beef. It lays a large, greenish-colored egg, about two-thirds the size of that of the ostrich.

It is very fleet of foot, and cannot easily be overtaken by either dogs or horses; as for man, it laugheth at *him*.

THE EMU, OR NEW HOLLAND CASSOWARY.

THE VICTORIAN EMU.

NOTE.—Neither this nor the preceding picture is a perfect representation of those we saw. The first more nearly resembles the body, the second the legs, neck and head, of the Victorian emu.

If a man undertakes to follow it on foot, he soon finds himself emu-*lating* at a rapid rate.

It is a mild, inoffensive bird, yet, when attacked, it kicks with such force as to kill a dog, or seriously injure a man; that is very like a mule.

The bird is rapidly disappearing. To obtain their eggs, which are in considerable demand in Melbourne, hunters need to go back far into the interior.

It will ultimately disappear from the Australian continent.

THE BAT.

There are no less than twenty-five different kinds of bats. Chief among these is the flying fox. This animal compares for size with the black squirrel of Canada. The color of its fur is about that of the red fox. It has also the fox's head and the same sly, cunning expression.

Its natural position when at rest is head downwards, with its wings wrapped about it like a lady's gossamer, and the two hooks or claws at the lower extremity of the wings hooked over a small limb.

It may rain a week, it is all the same to him. With his chin tucked close down upon his breast, every part of his body is protected from the weather, and so, if it is inclined to rain, why, he just hangs on, and "*lets it rain.*"

I touched him very gently with my cane. He dropped his nose downwards, that is, raised it upwards, and opened those cunning little eyes, as if to ask, "What do you want, sir? Have you anything for me to eat?" And then he put his chin back where it was, quite unconcernedly, leaving us to admire his shining black waterproof gossamer.

These animals, as also some others of the great bat tribe, are a perfect pest to growers of fruit. Nocturnal in their habits, they come down on the trees while men sleep, so that it is difficult to guard against them.

THE DUCK-BILLED PLATYPUS.

Of all the queer animals in Australia, the duck-billed platypus is the most so.

This is the link (or one of them) between the birds and the beasts. It is about eighteen inches long, and of a dark brown color. Its shape and its habits are very much like that of the otter. Its fur is very much finer; in fact, its fur is probably the finest and thickest of any animal known.

A coat or cloak made of platypus fur would be valued at not less than eighty or one hundred pounds, that is, four or five hundred dollars. Through the kindness of a friend, we were able to bring with us two skins as curios.

It eats frogs, mollusks, and water insects.

It has the bill of the duck, and lays eggs, from which its young are hatched, and suckles its young after hatching, till they are able to do for themselves. You have, therefore, in the platypus a strange commingling of the bird and the beast.

THE FLORA OF AUSTRALIA.

AS with the fauna so with the flora of Australia, quite unlike almost all other parts of the world, some thousands of species of flowering plants and trees have been discovered.

The wattle, of which there are several varieties, is very beautiful when in full bloom. We were fortunate in having an opportunity to see these trees at the flowering season in our drives through the country.

You find here, also, the magnificent acacias, yellow-flowered mimosa, sweet-scented myall, and flowering banksias.

Much of the scrub which covers the sandy plains presents, in the spring, a great variety of blossom. Many of these are armed with thick, short, sharp thorns and spikes, permitting you to admire their proteges (the flowers) with your eyes, but not to touch them with your hands. In almost all instances where we attempted to pluck wild native flowers we were met with these terrible thorns.

In the forests are the gigantic ferns; some of these grow to a height of forty and fifty feet. I presume

AUSTRALIAN FERN TREES.

Australasia, in which New Zealand is included, can present a greater and more beautiful variety of ferns than any other part of the world. The variety includes many hundreds.

We visited the Horticultural Gardens of Auckland, Melbourne, Sydney, Adelaide, Geelong, and Ballarat, besides having an opportunity, to some extent, to see them in their native condition.

Although for general building purposes the forests of Australia are not equal to those of Canada, for bridges and foundation work, where strength and endurance are demanded, the woods of the former country are equal, if not superior, to those of the latter.

THE EUCALYPTUS TREE.

The prevailing wood of Australia is the eucalyptus, of which there are many varieties, some say over one hundred. The "white gum," "red gum," and "shelly bark" are the larger kinds. Some of these grow to an immense size and height. One mighty giant measured, when prostrate, four hundred and eighty feet. Trees three hundred feet high are very common in the Gippsland country (eastern part of Victoria). These trees all exude a kind of gum (hence the name "gum," so largely applied to them), such as may frequently be seen upon a cherry or plum tree.

Like all other native trees in Australia, they shed their bark, and not their leaves. All trees of native growth in Australia are evergreen. When a thrifty "white gum," standing out in the pasture lands, has shed its coat for the season, and freshened up its leaves after the cooler, rainy season has fairly set in, it is very pretty. Those seen through the country generally are, however, rather of a stunted kind, and in the distance very much resemble our Canadian second growth oak.

One must go to the forest, and especially into those rainier and cooler regions to get a view of them when they reach their very best condition.

The white gum is, as a general rule, very straight-grained and can be rived out into pickets or shingles almost as smooth as if run out with a saw. These are largely used for palings, and sometimes are laid, clap-board fashion, on sheds and out-houses, or more frequently on settlers' shanties. In Australia, where the climate is much milder than in Canada, a tight wall is not so great a necessity.

The red gum is much more gnarled and durable. Fencing posts will last longer than cedar, though they are not nearly so easy to handle, being, like all other Australian woods, very heavy. It is said that none of these woods will float if thrown into the water. I have seen this statement contradicted. One thing I particularly noticed, however, was when we visited saw-mills on the Murray, the logs were brought down the river to the mill in barges, a thing that would never be thought of in Canada.

There are two very remarkable peculiarities belonging to the leaves of these eucalyptus trees. The leaves when young, say up to two or three months after appearing, are of a totally different shape from the older leaf.

It has lately been discovered that in botanical classification in Europe, several serious blunders have been made, through a lack of knowledge, of this peculiarity.

The young leaf has no resemblance whatever to the older one. When I first noticed it, in those cases where a shoot had started out from the body of the tree near the ground, I thought a vine or creeper of some sort had begun to wind itself about the tree, never for a moment thinking that both kinds of leaf belonged to the same tree. When specimens were collected for sending home to Europe, the persons who made the collections either failed to notice the difference in these leaves or failed to report, and the result is, confusion has already arisen which can only be corrected by the entire list of varieties being gone over again. The young leaf, which has all the appearance of being fully matured, is somewhat heart-shaped and thick or plump, and is an inch or an inch and a half wide and about as long, while the old leaf is long, narrow and thin, very much the shape of the peach leaf, only longer and thinner. The two resemble each other about as much as the fat, chubby hand of a plump baby, and the fourth finger on the hand of a tall, delicate lady.

The other peculiarity of the eucalyptus leaf is that, instead of hanging horizontally on the tree, it turns its edge to the sun. Someone had made up a jingling rhyme respecting the strange contradictions to be seen in nature in *terra antipodæ*, and this line occurs, which was quite a puzzle to us at the time:

"Where leaves have neither upper side nor under."

We were at a loss to know what that could possibly mean, until we had become familiar with the eucalyptus.

The eucalyptus is not so good a shade-tree as the English elm or oak, which grow very luxuriantly in Australian soil, yet it is planted in considerable numbers about residences and towns, because of its medicinal properties, being, as it is thought, a valuable preventive against all kinds of fever.

The oil extracted from the leaves is very extensively used throughout Australia, and is unquestionably a most valuable remedy. We have used it for a year or more, and consider it, whether for outward or inward application, much superior to anything of the kind we had ever before used.

THE WATTLE TREE.

The principal use made of the wattle tree is for tanning purposes. The bark is probably the most powerful astringent in the world, that is, regarding them in their simple, natural condition.

Extensive groves are planted for the tannan.

What is most strange is the fact that the young tree, two or three inches thick, stripped of its bark, continues to live, and will, in a short time recover its bark, to be stripped again.

THE NATIVE CHERRY TREE.

The native cherry is in appearance not quite so much like the English cherry, as chalk is like cheese. It is, when healthy and growing, very symmetrical and pretty, especially at a little distance from you. It has no leaves, but spines instead. These are coarser than those of the pine, and much rougher. The only reason why it is called *cherry* is because of its fruit, which is, after all, more unlike than like our cherry.

The slight resemblance, however, gives it the name. The fruit is red and is about the size of a cherry. It is white inside, dry and mealy, but, strange to say, has its stone on the outside.

SIGNS OF PROGRESS.

IN no part of the British Empire has there been more rapid growth in all the essential elements of civilization and national prosperity than in Australasia.

GROWTH OF POPULATION FROM 1873 TO 1885.

	1873.	1885.
Victoria	772,039	991,869
New South Wales	553,833	957,914
Queensland	146,690	315,489
South Australia	198,075	313,423
West Australia	25,761	35,186
Tasmania	104,217	133,791
New Zealand	295,946	575,226
	2,096,561	3,322,898
		2,096,561
Increase		1,226,337

An addition of over a million and a quarter, *i.e.*, over fifty per cent., in twelve years to the population of a country so young as Australasia must be regarded as very satisfactory.

With very rare exceptions this increase, as well as the previous population, is English-speaking, and solidly British. The foreigner has not yet found his way to Australasia to any great extent.

ANNUAL TRADE, INCLUDING BOTH IMPORTS AND EXPORTS, FROM 1873 TO 1885.

	1873.	1885.
Victoria	£31,836,310	£33,596,362
New South Wales	22,904,217	39,906,941
Queensland	6,428,012	11,665,894
South Australia	8,428,959	11,184,658
West Australia	562,546	1,097,083
Tasmania	2,000,723	3,071,179
New Zealand	12,075,058	14,299,860
	£84,235,825	£114,821,977

The above figures represent a growth of trade that is most encouraging. It is true that the balance of trade is as yet on the wrong side, the imports in all the colonies considerably exceeding the exports. There has been also a large increase of public debt in each colony. As an offset to both there are very extensive internal improvements, not so much of an unremunerative sort as arsenals, fortifications and the like, but railways, water-works, telegraphic and telephonic systems, which are principally in the hands of the Government, and are becoming, in some of the colonies at least, very remunerative.

Victoria could at any time, if she wished, dispose of her railways in the English market and wipe out at once her colonial debt. She would not, however, consider that a profitable transaction.

GROWTH OF RAILWAYS.

	1873.	1885.
Victoria	458	1676
New South Wales	397	1777
Queensland	218	1434
South Australia	202	1063
West Australia	30	184
Tasmania	45	257
New Zealand	145	1654
	1,495	8,045

New lines are being built. There are, at the time of this writing, not less than 10,000 miles in operation.

The telegraph system has grown in proportion to the growth of the railway system.

CULTIVATION OF THE SOIL.

If we turn to the cultivation of the land, and cereals and animal production, we find quite as rapid an increase.

The total number of acres under cultivation in all the colonies in 1873 was 3,306,923, while in 1885 we find the number of cultivated acres is 8,028,551, an increase of nearly five millions in twelve years.

The average yield per acre is not equal to that of Canada. This is partly to be accounted for by the lack of rain through much of the year.

Taking the whole country, I do not think the average acre is equal in productive strength to that of Canada. There are portions of Victoria, however, especially in the south-west, which probably cannot be surpassed in the whole world for strength of soil. The continuous yield of that part of the colony is something enormous, and I dare say the same may be said of portions of other colonies. I am inclined to think, however, that the Canadian soil is much superior, taking into account the whole territory.

On the other hand, the mildness of the climate gives the Australian farmer the advantage in the longer ploughing season, enabling him to cultivate a much larger acreage, as there is no frost to interfere with his tillage

The mode of farming in Australia differs very much from that of the Old World. A farmer with the aid of only one hired man, except for a few days in harvest time, can put in and harvest 200 or, in some instances, 300 acres in a season. As there is no necessity for housing stock, the straw is not gathered. The grain is taken by means of strippers, and the ploughing is largely done by gang ploughs. This will explain why it is that an average yield of six or seven bushels per acre pays expenses and yields a profit besides.

The extensive fields of wheat as seen in Australia in October and November, reaching over the wide plains or undulating uplands, constitute one of the interesting sights of the country.

The grain ripens the latter part of November and early part of December, and the rapidity with which it ripens in that dry climate taxes the fullest capacity of the farmer and his family while the harvest operations last.

In 1873 Australasia produced $18\frac{1}{4}$ millions of bushels of wheat, and in 1885 the yield had risen to $32\frac{1}{4}$ millions. The yield of potatoes in the latter year amounted to 410,000 tons, and of hay, 1,064,000 tons. Hay and chaff in Australia are two things entirely different from what is meant by these words with us. Hay is not cured English or native grass. It is wheat or oats, and sometimes other grains, but principally these, harvested just before ripe, when the grain is about full grown, but while the husk is still firm enough to retain its hold upon the grain. It is usually bound into sheaves and left in the field till thoroughly dried, then stacked and later on is chopped fine with a "cutting box" and put into bags; this fine-cut, unthreshed grain is called "chaff." Almost every town or village has its "chaff mills." Some of these do a large business putting up *chaff* for India.

The farmers very frequently find it much more profitable to turn the wheat crop into hay than to allow it to ripen.

It is very remarkable that the English grasses do not thrive in Australia, as a general rule. There is not, however, the same necessity that they should as with us, for the climate is so mild that very little stock, except working horses, are stabled. For these the chaff, as described above, is a more convenient fodder than that of the North, where the horse must be supplied three times a day with grain in addition to his hay supply. The dried native grass is often used for bedding, as there is very little straw, the ripe wheat being largely gathered with " strippers " by which only the heads are taken.

LIVE STOCK.

The number of horses possessed by the colonies in 1873 was something less than a million ; now there are about one and a half millions;

In 1873 there were upon the pastures 3,844,000 head of cattle. The number, in 1885, had risen to 8,260,000. I am told that the rearing of a steer to three or four years old, on Australian pastures, is only a matter of a few shillings expense. If the water supply during those years is fairly good, a few thousands of such stock are a rich harvest for their owners.

The chief difficulty and danger is the uncertainty of the rains. Drought in New South Wales or Queensland means not only much suffering on the part of the poor beasts, but much loss. There has been, so far, however, much more to encourage than to discourage, or we should not have the record of this large increase of production.

In 1873 the several colonies had on their "*runs*" fifty-six and three-quarter millions of sheep. During the twelve years under consideration the number had increased to eighty-four and a quarter millions.

There are many other sources of wealth, and other evidences of growth, which I shall not enumerate.

THE GOLD PRODUCT OF AUSTRALASIA.

Few countries anywhere on the globe can present a better record of material prosperity. I must, however, give the reader some account of that attractive element which brought, originally, to these shores such vast numbers from the Old World.

The production of gold in all the Australasian colonies, since that metal was first discovered in 1851, down to 1888, is in round numbers 80,000,000 ounces, worth, say, £500,000,000 sterling, which, reckoned at $5 to the pound, would give us $1,500,000,000. Of this the mines in the colony of Victoria have produced considerably more than one-half.

Immense nuggets have been found in past years,

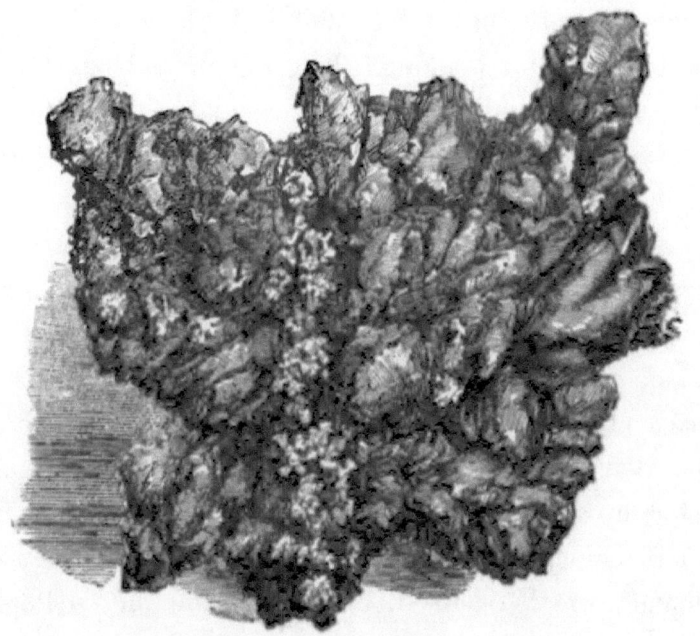

THE GOLD NUGGET, "WELCOME STRANGER,"
Found near Dunolly, 1869. Weight, 2,248 ounces; value, about $50,000.

some of them upon the surface. Above is a cut of a large one, which, like many others, has an interesting history.

In many cases poor men, who have been reduced

almost to beggary and starvation, wandering listlessly about, knowing not where to seek for the precious metal, their efforts so frequently failing, have stubbed their toes against just such a pile of wealth as you see in this " welcome stranger." A party had excavated some distance into a hill, and had for several days carted earth for washing. In going in and out they had used a boulder (which was inconvenient to lift out of their way) as a step down from the outside into their drift. A circus had come into the town, and most of the men had gone to the show. One preferred to remain and dig. There had been a heavy rain, which had washed everything within its reach pretty clean, and just as the man was returning from the excavation with his load of dirt, he noticed something peculiar in the stone on which they all had been stepping up and down for several days. Examining it more closely, he discovered that it was an immense nugget, worth twenty-five or thirty thousand dollars, or more.

One could fill a whole volume with just such finds.

There are also tales to be told which give quite a different shading to the picture. Some who become suddenly rich become almost as suddenly poor, by making big ventures for larger riches. Others lost all by giving themselves up to the wildest extravagance.

Nine-pins were played with bottles of champagne, for which he who broke fewest had to pay.

"Treating the crowd," which is commonly known in Australia as "shouting," sometimes cost the individual *hundreds of pounds*.

One very lucky fellow, who afterwards came to poverty, had his horse shod with gold.

In many instances drunkenness brought to disgrace and utter poverty and rags men who had made thousands of pounds in the gold mines.

Surface diggings and nuggets are not much thought of now, as they seem to have been almost wholly exhausted. About all the gold mining done in the country now is in quartz, for which large capital and costly machinery must be obtained, as the gold must now be sought deep down beneath the surface. We were in one of these 500 feet. After reaching the bottom, we went nearly a half mile in the drift. The gentleman who accompanied us very kindly explained all the mysteries and uncertainties of gold mining. The process is too long for explanation here.

It is better for such broad, rich territories as Australia, when its inhabitants settle down into the steady development of the general natural resources which are presented other than gold, as seeking for that element is usually attended with undue and unhealthy excitement. Australia has vast wealth independent of her gold. We will turn for a little to other evidences of prosperity not solely of a material kind, although partly the result of it.

POSTAL STATISTICS.

The number of letters despatched and received at the post-offices of Australasia for 1884 was 138,103,105, and the number of newspapers 72,974,632. The rapid growth may be seen if we take the figures for Victoria for illustration :

	Letters.	Newspapers.
1851	504,425	456,741
1861	6,109,929	4,277,179
1871	11,716,166	5,172,970
1881	26,308,347	11,440,732
1885	36,061,880	16,277,108

The growth in most of the other colonies is even larger, the number of letters passing through the New South Wales post-offices for 1884 being 42,237,000, and the number of newspapers 25,063,500.

PUBLIC LIBRARIES.

In almost every town we visited we found a well-furnished Mechanics' Institute and Public Library. In this respect the Australians do themselves great credit, and set an example worthy of imitation.

PUBLIC LIBRARIES. 123

The buidings of the Melbourne Public Library have cost in all £112,000. The number of books in the Melbourne Library is about 50,000. If to these we add pamphlets and other periodicals we have **174,380**. It is open to the public, without payment, from ten

LIBRARY OF MELBOURNE.

a.m. to ten p.m., and is visited by over 325,000 persons per year.

Throughout the colony of Victoria, over which we travelled so largely, there are 280 of these useful institutions, the number of volumes in them all amounting to 353,000, while the number of visits paid them during the year was over three millions.

BOTANICAL AND HORTICULTURAL GARDENS.

The Australians have shown commendable spirit and enterprise in the formation of botanical and horticultural gardens. There is scarcely a town of any size which has not at least a botanical garden, and everywhere we went we found public parks set apart and adorned with native and foreign trees and shrubbery.

I think in this respect the Australians outdo all peoples whom I know.

These lines are written not so much to praise as to, if possible, stimulate others, but especially Canadians, for I fear we are far behind in this respect.

The city of Melbourne, including its suburbs, has no less than seventy-eight parks and public gardens, embracing in all 5,101 acres. The Royal Park has 444 acres, Botanic Gardens, 235, Fitzroy Garden, immediately in rear of Parliament buildings, has sixty-four acres. This park is most beautifully kept.

Statuary adorns all the walks, foreign and native trees are all luxuriant. Roses are almost always in bloom. The ferns in the low valley tempt you to halt for a little and admire their lovely fronds.

When one is tired with the toil of the day and choked with the dust of the city, he is rested while

FITZROY GARDEN, MELBOURNE.

he strolls down these beautiful walks and breathes the pure air of the park.

When you visit Melbourne, do not forget the parks and gardens.

The mildness of the climate, of course, gives our antipodean cousins a very great advantage over us, as very few, if any, of the park plants or flowers have to be housed for the winter. Making all allowance for this difference, however, the Canadians are still far behind in their efforts in this direction.

Horticultural societies are encouraged by the Government, and are found now in almost all parts of the land.

The Royal Horticultural Society of Victoria, located at Melbourne, is the oldest and most important. It has five hundred members. We visited their garden in Richmond Park, accompanied by one of the directors, a very dear friend, M. L. Hutchinson, Esq.

The collection of fruit trees is very large.

There are in this garden over six hundred different kinds of apple trees, ninety different kinds of cherries, twenty-eight of currant, one hundred and twenty of gooseberries, twenty-one of oranges, four hundred pears, one hundred and two peaches, one hundred and forty-eight plums, fifty strawberries, one hundred and seventy grapes, eighteen raspberries, forty-eight apricots, fifty-six figs. New varieties are annually imported from Europe, America, Japan, and other countries.

CHURCHES AND COLLEGES.

The number of churches in the colony of Victoria for 1855 was 349; for 1865 it was 1,695; for 1875 it was 2,519; for 1885 it was 3,982.

The increase in the number of churches and chapels is greater than the increase of population. Victoria may be said to be very well supplied with churches, as there is offered by these nearly 4,000 buildings to a population of one million—room for all.

Counting one hundred and twenty-five as a fair average congregation, you have a seating capacity for 500,000 persons, which is as large a percentage of the people as could reasonably be expected to attend service upon any given day.

I doubt whether any country in the old world could give us a more favorable showing as regards provision for the spiritual wants of the population.

The number of Sabbath-schools in 1884 was 2,044; in 1885 the number had increased to 2,157. The children attending these schools is about 150,000.

The Methodist denomination return the largest number, viz.: 39,675. Next to them the Presbyterians,

29,710; next to them, Church of England, 27,903, and next, Roman Catholic, 23,751.

The day-schools also show a satisfactory growth.

The Melbourne University is worthy of at least a short notice. Its foundation-stone was laid in 1854. Royal letters patent were granted, giving it university powers in 1859. In 1880 it was thrown open to ladies, admitting them to all its corporate privileges.

Provision having been made for the establishment of affiliated colleges in connection with the religious denominations, the Church of England has erected Trinity College, the Presbyterians Ormond College, and the Wesleyans Queen's College, all quite near the University. We had the privilege of witnessing the laying of the foundation-stone of the last named, by Sir Henry Loch. Lady Loch, and Lady Brassey, of the *Sunbeam*, being also on the platform to witness the ceremony.

Up to 1886 there were, in round numbers, twelve hundred graduates from the several departments, and very nearly four hundred and fifty matriculants were on their way towards graduation.

As a colonial institution the Melbourne University ranks high, being held quite equal to the universities of England.

MELBOURNE COFFEE PALACES.

AMONG the factors at work in the direction of the restriction and diminution of the liquor traffic in Australia, are the great coffee palaces or temperance hotels which have lately been erected, together with others which are being erected, not merely in Melbourne, but in various parts of the country. The question has been asked, Can hotels be successfully run without the sale of intoxicants? These magnificent hotels, so thoroughly equipped, and so acceptable to the public and remunerative to investors, are answering that question in a most satisfactory way.

That there must be places for the entertainment of the travelling public everybody admits. That these places must sell intoxicants in order to live and flourish a great many good people deny. Many of these houses which sell intoxicants are, by reason of such sale, public nuisances, and not a public necessity. Even the best of them are less useful, as regards their service to mankind, because of such sale.

The bars of some of these very respectable hotels are frequently the starting point towards ruin for

FEDERAL COFFEE PALACE OR TEMPERANCE HOTEL, MELBOURNE.

young men, who could not be induced to begin an evil course at a brothel or a mere grog-shop.

Besides, no matter how well managed these houses may be, some one who has formed the drink habit is sure to get at them that which turns him into a semi-idiot for the time being, and then, between his blasphemy and his incoherent and half-formed sentences, and his over-friendliness, he becomes a positive nuisance to decent people. I have seen this over and over again at some of "the very best hotels."

Even drinkers in a moderate way hate this sort of thing, and very much prefer hotels where they will not be disturbed by such experiences.

The managers of the coffee palaces in Melbourne tell me that quite one-half, or even more than a half, of their large patronage is from persons who are not teetotallers. They prefer hotels where liquor is not sold.

I had the opportunity, in 1886, of looking into the cocoa rooms system in Liverpool. There were at that time sixty-three of these places of entertainment. They had 27,000 patrons daily.

By means of this system the poor laborer could get a mug of coffee for a ha'penny, a sandwich for a penny, or a very good substantial dinner for sixpence, while at the same time he could have a seat and a table if he desired to bring with him his own luncheon.

The sale of beer and other liquors in the city of Liverpool has been greatly reduced in this way, and many a poor man been saved from the formation of the drinking habit, because saved from the dangerous influences of the tap-room.

The system was begun by philanthropic men, who invested in it from pure philanthropic motives. To their great surprise, it has turned out to be a thoroughly good investment, while, as a business transaction in the fullest sense of the word, it treats the poor man as a man, and not as a pauper.

These noble men who first inaugurated the system are sometimes twitted by the opponents of temperance respecting their "ten per cent." philanthropy. But a philanthropy which brings ten per cent. is a deal more honorable than a business which, besides its large profits, is a system of the meanest and worst form of robbery—robbing men of their time, their respectability, their morals, and innocent women and children of even bread itself.

THE FEDERAL COFFEE PALACE.

It is very remarkable that the Coffee Palace system of Melbourne was originated in the same spirit as that to which I have referred above, with the result precisely the same. I am indebted to the Melbourne

Daily Telegraph for the following description of the Federal Coffee Palace, a picture of which is given on a preceding page. This magnificent structure was being erected during our stay in Melbourne and Victoria, and in my addresses throughout the colony I found it an advantage to point my hearers to it and others like it, as Melbourne's reply to the statement that first-class hotels could not be run without intoxicants. Our Victorian friends have set the whole world an example in this respect.

"There could not be a better proof of the unprecedented advancement Melbourne has made than in its immense hotels—great palatial structures which rival even the famous 'Grands,' 'Langhams,' and 'Burlingtons' of the Old World, and the vast edifices of the United States. Where there is a large manufacturing and mining population, and an uninterrupted flow of travellers from all countries, there is necessarily much prosperity, and Melbourne peculiarly is an instance of this. Enterprise has secured from sojourners, for the metropolis of Australia, the name of the most comfortable city in the southern continent, and, indeed, in none of the other capitals can the casual visitor find his wants nearly so well supplied. A suggestion of philanthropists resulted in the establishment of coffee palaces, intended originally as a corrective to the baneful effect of the number of drinking shops with which the city unfortunately abounds. Coffee palaces, originally, were for the working and laboring classes: they were to provide these important members of the community with means for recreation, to become popular resorts, but nearly everybody knows how it was that object failed almost from its inception. From small establishments the palaces grew almost instantaneously to something more worthy of their name; shrewd business men began to see that the new idea would, properly carried out, be productive of large dividends, and the 'boons to workingmen' became colossal hotels conducted on the temperance principle. In the heart of Melbourne, upon land which had reached a fabulous value, the Victoria Club was transformed into the Victoria Coffee Palace. Then there rose in Bourke Street the Melbourne Coffee Palace, another gigantic edifice of many floors. Then the Grand Hotel, a building worthy of its title, was erected in Spring Street, and though it did not answer all expectations at first, men of business saw in it future fortunes, and it passed into their hands. Then it became the Grand Coffee Palace, and instantaneously prosperity commenced. To meet the growing want the Federal Coffee Palace was projected by James Mirams, M.P. As a coffee palace, it is the

THE FEDERAL COFFEE PALACE.

largest affair of the kind in the world; as an hotel, it is second to very few. The company which has brought it into existence was formed during May and June, 1885, and it was registered on the 29th of July, the following month. Some particulars of the eagerness manifested for the stock will show the opinion held by the general public of the investment. The capital is £100,000, in 100,000 shares of £1 each, and the first issue closed on the 2nd November, 1885, at which time 59,921 shares had been allotted. The list was closed until the 14th of December in the same year, and 16,268 shares were taken up at their full price before it was again closed on the 11th March last.

. . . .

"It might almost be called a triumph of the art of the architect and the skill of the builder, and it can readily be understood that so large an amount as £13,000 was required for the foundations which carry the thousands upon thousands of bricks and the massive pillars which go to complete the building. The style of architecture is not easily described. It comprises a little of everything—Corinthian, Ionic, Doric, early English, late English, Queen Anne, Elizabethan and Australian—in fact, it may be called the last Though so great it is not heavy, and if the walls be massive, they answer the dual purpose of preserving warmth in the cold months and keeping out the heat of summer. These features should be in every hotel, and the directors and architects of the Federal Coffee Palace have done wisely in ensuring them. There are three entrances, one on the corner and one each in King and Collins' Streets. Fluted Corinthian pillars rise on each side of it to a height of between twenty feet and thirty feet, and hold a massive cornice, on which is a motto, 'Restez Ici,' with a similar invitation in German. From this entrance the grand staircase is reached. This is of veined marble, and the effect of such very fine stone, with the most brilliant white of plastered walls, make the effect palatial indeed. The grand staircase leads to corridors, from which access may be had to any portion of the building, but it is not the only means of ascent and descent. Half a dozen other staircases, all of stone and fireproof, provide greater facilities, and the fast travelling American lifts, which latterly have come so much into favor, afford additional comfort and safety. At the corner entrance are the offices of the managers, and apart from the shops in King and Collins' Streets, nearly the whole of the remainder of ground floor is taken up by the public dining saloon. Like the palace itself, this is on a great scale, as can be imagined when it is stated that from 600 to 700 persons can be seated at one time. Much care has been devoted to the decoration of this hall; the pillars have exercised all the ingenuity of modellers, and are dadoed and frescoed in accordance with all the requirements of high art.

"Part of the duty of the management will be to ensure a rapid service to customers; indeed, such will be a necessity, and to thoroughly carry this out there are half a score of rapid lifts communicating with the domain of the cooks. The floor space is of dimensions sufficient to provide for a public billiard room, and a comfortable smoking room and lounge, fitted up in accordance with the rest of the institution. This much is for casual visitors, the lodgers and all such patrons of the hotel live in a world of their own in the upper stories. On the second floor they have their drawing rooms, reception rooms, breakfast and dining rooms, rooms where ladies and their friends may gossip over the five o'clock tea, sitting rooms, lounges, and a billiard room, every one of which will be directly lighted. Light and ventilation are features of the Federal Coffee Palace. Oriel and bay windows are numerous to increase the beauty of these apartments, and in each one there are ventilating shafts to carry away impure air. In this way a blast comes from below and sweeps the vitiated atmosphere above it through other shafts, until it is blown away from the roof. The choicest of the drawing rooms, as well as the private dining rooms, and the great restaurant below, are panelled in figured, mirrored, bevelled glass. The next floor, and the two others above it, are occupied by the bedrooms, of which there are no fewer than 450. Though this number seems great, the rooms themselves are much larger and higher than are generally found in hotels, and each suite has in conjunction with it marble baths and all other conveniences, fitted with continual supplies of hot water from a massive boiler, built in the basement. As below, direct light is studied, and one hundred electric bells place the residents in quick communication with the servants of the establishment. There certainly is no hotel in Australia so well designed, so large, or so convenient; and it is not altogether a boast on the part of the directors when they assert that there are not a dozen in the world superior to it. From its domes to its foundation it is a magnificent structure, and it stands as a wonderful instance of Melbourne's advancement, and a monument of the energy and skill of its founder, Mr. Mirams, and those who have been associated with him in the undertaking, whether as directors of the company, architects, or contractors."

That which makes the above deeply interesting is

the wonderful growth of temperance sentiment rendering the existence of such establishments possible.

Australia is beginning to realize, with the whole civilized world, that the liquor traffic is a disgrace to the civilization of the nineteenth century, and a curse to humanity as well as a continual insult to God; and our antipodean cousins are making most commendable efforts to oppose and restrict, with strong hope that they will at no very distant day abolish it.

There are many noble workers—hundreds, whom I should be glad to name if space permitted. The Rechabites are a strong body; the Good Templars, the Melbourne Total Abstinence Society, the Women's Christian Temperance Union, are all doing grand service and embrace hundreds of God's true nobility. The Victorian Alliance is the central organization in that colony (Victoria), which unites the various forces for legislative purposes. The very efficient Secretary, Mr. John Vale, has the rare faculty of winning the good will of all who love the temperance cause.

The Hon. James Munroe, the President of the Alliance, and Mr. J. W. Hunt, Chairman of the Committee, with our very dear friend, Mr. Gordon, M.P., formerly of Canada, are gentlemen who leave nothing undone to secure success in their noble and self-denying work.

With such men at the head, and with such enthusiastic workers as it was our good pleasure to meet in all parts of the country, what may we not expect in the prosecution of this great reform?

MONUMENT TO BURKE AND WILLS.

BURKE AND WILLS, THE EXPLORERS.

THERE is a class of men who are generally more deserving of our gratitude than we are apparently disposed to admit, at least in any practical way.

I mean those self-denying, adventurous men, pioneers and explorers, who, taking their lives in their hands, go forth to grapple with difficulties they know not what, that they may open the way for civilization, for settlement of uninhabited regions, for the amelioration of the condition of the savage, or to extend the field of scientific and Christian knowledge. Perhaps fully fifty per cent. or more of these courageous men pay the penalty with their lives. Who can help admiring the spirit of such men as Sir John Franklin, and Kane, and Rae, and others who have penetrated the frozen regions about and beyond the Arctic circle?

Or Speke, and Livingstone and Stanley, who have braved difficulties quite as great under the scorching rays of the equatorial sun?

Passing over these vast Atlantic and Pacific seas, in ships so well fitted up for the comfort of passengers, with accurate charts, and lighthoused capes, and islands of even a few acres all well known to the navigators of to-day, by which even circumnavigation of our globe is brought up to the pleasure of a picnic excursion, I cannot but wonder at and admire the intrepidity of such men as Columbus and Jacques Cartier, Dampier and Cook, and a host of others who have, by their self-sacrificing zeal, made known the existence of broad continents and islands innumerable, abounding with mineral wealth and fertile soil, with great rivers of pure water, magnificent scenery, with a boundless store of native fruits and animals, which the Divine Hand had supplied for the support and pleasure of civilized humanity or aboriginal tribes.

Among these worthies, the two men whose names are at the head of this chapter are deserving of a place. Their efforts may not have been on so extended a scale as some whom I have mentioned above, nor may the results have been equal. Their spirit was the same, however, and their end was that of many who have undertaken that kind of work—a work which must be done by some noble souls such as they, or our earth for the greater part might remain a vast howling wilderness forever.

While the coasts of Australia were well known, and the southern portions of the continent settled, towns and villages springing up everywhere, with millions of sheep and cattle on the frontier "runs," there were vast regions in the north which were as yet, even to the oldest Australian settler, a *terra incognita*. What is the nature of that great lone-land? Are there mountains, are there streams, vast prairies of rich grasses, innumerable game? Or are there parched, arid and sterile wastes of sand, where the traveller, as on the African deserts—footsore, wearied, hungered, but, most of all, athirst—stretches himself upon the sands to die, leaving his poor bones to be picked by the vultures, and bleached by the unpitying sun?

These were questions which awaited their answering. Who will venture to tell us all about this great unknown? A Mr. Kyte had offered £1,000 towards exploring the interior; the Victorians contributed handsomely; while the Government also was liberal in its offer to outfit an expedition. Wealthy men and busy merchants were ready in every possible way to encourage it, but who will face the responsibility of conducting an expedition so full of doubt and danger?

These brave men consented to assume command. Wills was a surveyor, a native of Geelong. Burke, an Irishman by birth, had been for some years a sub-inspector of police in Melbourne. Wills was the more highly educated and literary man of the two, though both were spirited and full of the true ambition.

As it had been suspected that there were parched sands and desert wastes through which they must pass to reach the northern coast, camels, twenty-seven in all, had been brought from India to carry through the desert the necessary stores.

The expedition set out from Melbourne August 20th, 1860. They went north a few hundred miles to Cooper's Creek, where they halted for a little, and after consultation erected a station, and stored the greater part of their provisions. Leaving a sufficient number in charge of the stores, the leaders started with one or two others on their perilous and trying journey. The distance to be traversed was much greater, and required much more time, than had been calculated upon by either division of the party. The leaders pushed forward, however, till they succeeded in reaching the Gulf of Carpentaria.

Long before they reached Cooper's Creek, on their return journey, their water and food supplies were done, and they themselves quite ready to die, not merely from hunger and thirst, but from fatigue, which was enough of itself to have overcome them, even if their supplies had been sufficient. They had been so long absent that the party in charge of the stores had quite given them up for lost, and breaking up their camp, they started south for Melbourne on the morning of the very day that the footsore and worn-out explorers returned to it.

Seeing the word "DIG" cut into a tree, they dug down only to find a bottle with a paper enclosed, telling them that the camp had been abandoned that very morning.

Wills was too much exhausted to proceed further. Burke, accompanied by King, one of their exploring companions, attempted to reach the settlement further south. The third day Burke died. King returned to the old camp, where he found poor Wills had also succumbed.

King succeeded in reaching friendly natives, who cared for his wants for many weeks, till he was able to make his way back to civilization, and make known the fate of his unfortunate leaders. To quote the words of Sir Henry Barkley, Governor of Victoria, "So fell two as gallant spirits as ever sacrificed their lives for the extension of science. Both men were in their prime, and both resigned comfort and competency to embark in this worthy enterprise."

A well-executed statue of these brave men, of which the cut at the head of this chapter is a picture, erected by the citizens of Melbourne, stands in one of the most beautiful parts of that great and growing city.

As the papers of the explorers were recovered, their work was a success, though it cost them so dearly.

PERILS OF PIONEERING.

I HAVE often in my boyhood listened to tales of adventure and hardship endured by the early pioneers of Canada, where frost and snow played a prominent part among the difficulties which our worthy fathers had to face.

I doubt, however, whether anything in the history of travel or adventure could surpass the following narrative, which I received from the lips of our much-loved friends, whose names are given below.

I never listened to anything more thrilling.

If Canada, with her severe winters, has her way of trying the early settler, Australia also has hers.

In North Queensland, where great suffering must sometimes be endured from drought and heat, there are now and then in the winter season rains that remind one of the days of Noah and his Ark.

Perhaps in no other country on this globe are there anywhere such rains as Queensland sometimes knows.

The reader will be interested in hearing what Messrs. Barber have to say about them in their descriptions of a journey of one hundred and seventy miles, between Rockhampton and Oakey Creek station, in North Queensland, made by Mr. and Mrs. G. P. Barber and Samuel Barber, on the occasion of their taking possession of a sheep station in that region :—

MR. G. P. BARBER'S DESCRIPTION.

We arrived at Rockhampton by steamer from Melbourne, March 11th, 1869. We had on board a new American express waggon, built for this journey. After much bargaining, we bought two harness horses and one saddle horse.

Having packed away our luggage and a supply of rations, and all necessary cooking utensils, with gun, axe, and tent, and a long list of sundries, making in all considerably over half a ton weight, we made a start for the Peak Downs, over unmade roads, bridgeless rivers, and a country infested by bush rangers. We were warned against camping near the Deep Creek, where a notorious gang was lurking.

Although in Queensland March is a part of the rainy season, at the time of our starting the weather was dry and the roads good, and there was no appearance of floods; but we had scarcely left Rockhampton when signs of a change were visible, and before reaching the Deep Creek, fifteen miles from town, the rain poured down, as it only can in the tropics, making the soft black soil exceedingly heavy to drag over, and great difficulty was experienced in crossing the Deep Creek, as the opposite bank was very steep, soft and slippery

THIS IS HOW IT RAINS IN QUEENSLAND.

from the wet. However, the top was reached, but the horses were by this time so fagged that we determined to unyoke for the night, hoping for better weather on the morrow.

On one side of the track was a flat of some hundreds of acres, covered with native flax, growing in wild luxuriance eight feet high, and forming an almost impenetrable forest. On the other side of the track was a grassy slope, where we hoped our horses would be content.

Having hobbled and belled them, we prepared our evening repast, which was eaten under difficulties, as the tropical rain still descended, wetting our clothes, and giving us discomfort on every side. However, we had light hearts, and made the best of everything, and soon endeavored to forget our troubles in sleep. My wife and I settled down inside the waggon, which was covered with a canvas tilt, while my brother Sam, finding it impracticable to pitch his tent in mud and water, crawled under the conveyance and, without undressing, rolled himself up in his blanket, and thus sought rest from the cares of this lower world.

His slumbers were but short, as the bells from the horses told us they were wandering, and had entered the forest of native flax; so, hastening after them, and after floundering about in the darkness, and being drenched to the skin, he succeeded in bringing them back. The next morning showed no improvement in the weather, but we tried to proceed. Our horses were, however, unable to move the load, the wheels being clogged with black clay, up to the axles. The day was spent in trying to buy another horse, which we succeeded in doing; but the time was so far gone that we stayed another night.

On the morrow we dragged heavily along; the rain still kept on, causing us to fear that the river Fitzroy at Yaamba, twenty-five miles from Rockhampton, would be flooded. Fortunately we succeeded in fording this large river just in time. The water, fast rising, necessitated unloading the waggon, and packing the goods on the horses. The packages got partially wet, but not much damaged. The township of Yaamba supplied us with various necessaries of life, and we thoroughly enjoyed a good dinner, after the rough camping out in mud and water.

Proceeding on our journey, we called on an old settler, a Mr. Vickary, who, being exceedingly hospitable, insisted on our stopping at his comfortable homestead. We bought of him another horse and harness, and yoked three in the waggon for future travelling. Our progress was slow and tedious, owing to the soft state of the country, the waggon leaving tracks like plough furrows in the wet, black soil.

We duly reached Marlborough township, sixty miles from Rockhampton, the weather being still very unsettled, and we feared floods in the next river which ran between us and our future home. We made forced marches, and frequently reached our camp after dark, when fuel and grass had to be found, supper cooked, and blankets dried. Our slow progress had caused our rations to run short, and no store being near, we were threatened with famine. A fortnight of toiling brought us to the banks of the river Mackenzie, which, to our dismay, we found in full flood. We determined to run up the Mackenzie, and cross at the junction of the Isaacs river.

Our home lay forty miles beyond this point, and, if we were only across the water, could be reached in a day, and our troubles would be over. But there flowed the surging river, which drains an area of country equal to all Scotland. Our rations done and no supplies obtainable, the question was, What was to be done? The country is very sparsely populated, and many cattle stations are forty miles apart. We passed one family of kind-hearted Scotch people, who were quite willing to supply our wants, but unfortunately their ration teams were delayed with the floods, and they were as badly off as ourselves.

We found there was a custom of crossing the rivers in bark canoes, formed of large sheets of bark stripped from gum trees, fastened at the ends, and made watertight with stiff clay. We determined to make such a canoe and cross the flood, swim the horses over, and proceed on horseback. We started to swim the horses, but the poor brutes refused to cross the torrent, and, in spite of all entreatings and urgings, would not breast the tide. We then decided to leave waggon, baggage, and horses, cross ourselves, and travel on foot to Columbra, ten miles from the river.

Having made a canoe, and placed a few necessaries therein, my brother and I made the first voyage, and succeeded in reaching the other side. I returned for my wife. The second journey was begun; and, after placing an old air-jacket which, although defective, contained sufficient air to keep one afloat for a few minutes, a single paddle was used to propel the canoe. And now a misfortune happened, which placed our lives in extreme jeopardy. The flood had submerged snags and saplings, and, passing over one of these, the paddle was entangled, and in an instant was jerked from my hand. We were now at the mercy of the foaming torrent. The canoe whirled round and round, in the eddyings of the current, and was swiftly borne down the stream, rushing past trees which threatened our destruction. My brother was left behind a mile, when our frail bark dashed against a tree, and commenced to sink.

Foreseeing the catastrophe, I divested myself of all

clothing except a Crimean shirt, and seizing the rein of a bridle, we clung to the weak bough of an oak tree which was unsteadily swaying in the current. This refuge was very unsafe, and a better tree was descried some six or seven yards away. To reach this I swam, bearing up my wife, having her neckerchief in my teeth. My wife got under water several times, but the tree was reached, which, however, was found to be but little better than the first, and another tree was chosen as a safer refuge still further on. This swim was accomplished by the bridle rein being fastened one end around my wife's waist, and the other end round over my shoulder, my "better half" floating behind. This was much more successful, and a strong oak was reached with a stout bough a little above water level. It was now six o'clock in the evening, and the prospect was not cheering, there being only room for one on this bough. I climbed some twelve feet higher, and on another bough I spent the night.

It might be thought that, in such a sorry plight, our feelings would be gloomy, but our youthful spirits and British pluck were equal to the occasion, and although hungry and weary, with our lives in imminent peril, myself with only a shirt on, and wife with hat lost and clothes bedraggled, we passed the night clinging to this oak, singing all the hymns and songs we could remember to prevent us from falling asleep and dropping into the surging flood beneath us.

During the night several thunderstorms passed over us, with drenching rain, but, strange to say, neither flood nor lightning flash caused us fear, and in early dawn we held a council as to what was to be done. I offered my wife an alternative, of being again strapped behind me while we swam for the shore, or being left on the tree while I swam ashore to get help to rescue her. Extreme danger lay in either plan. I might be lost, and never return with help, in which case my wife must remain on the tree to starve, or become exhausted and drop into the roaring torrent below us; while, if we tried to swim together, it was very doubtful if my strength was equal to the task, as after starving and exposure, I felt in a very weak state. I was so cold that my teeth chattered as I talked, but one or the other plan must be faced, there was no escape from that.

My wife elected to be strapped to her liege lord, and, seeing that this was in our honeymoon, it was most befitting, if we had so soon to die, that we should be tied together in the last struggle. But it pleased a kind Providence to order differently. The strap was adjusted, and the moment for the final plunge arrived, a short prayer rose to Heaven, and we were again in the rushing tide. My first sensation was warmth and strength—the water being warmer than the night air so nourished my system that I felt like a giant in strength, and almost supernatural power was experienced in dragging my young wife through the surging river.

A difficulty was seen ahead, for a sharp bend in the river had caused a whirlpool, which had excavated the bank, leaving a perpendicular wall some forty feet high. A glance into this whirlpool convinced me that to enter it would be certain death, and the only escape lay in slightly stemming the tide, and landing higher up. This caused much extra exertion, and before reaching land my wife was pulled several times under water, which almost took away her hope of being saved. Providentially, she retained perfect presence of mind all through this trying ordeal, or in all probability both would have met with a watery grave.

Our landing-place was quite unknown to us, as the current had borne us, when in the canoe, beyond the junction of the Isaacs and the Mackenzie rivers. A dense scrub presented itself to us. My first thought was to find my brother, but, having passed the junction this was impossible. We next struck into the scrub, hoping to find a track to the Columbra cattle station, but the sun became obscured, and with nothing to guide us, we were soon travelling over our own tracks, when I knew it was hopeless to proceed. I now regretted having left the river, and we sat down on a fallen log, for the first time feeling dispirited.

After some time a glimpse of the sun was seen, and I at once took my bearings, and determined to return to the river, thinking more succour was to be found there than in the dreaded Briglow scrub. We were soon rewarded by hearing the roar of the river through the trees. Numerous tortoises jumped into the river at our approach. We now travelled down the course of the river, hoping to find some signs of civilization along the banks, where cattle stations were generally to be found. Our course was slow and tedious; dense scrub had to be forced through, and several creeks too deep to ford were met with; these had to be run up, and when shallow enough to cross, we passed over, and returned back to the river on the other side. A large lagoon was forded waist deep and then, to our delight, we saw a bush track, leading from the river to the scrub. Knowing that this must lead somewhere we followed it for two miles, when my wife was quite exhausted from fatigue and starvation.

A hill before us invited us onwards, and the bridle

rein, which I still retained, was once more brought into requisition—one end fastened round the wife's waist and the other over my shoulder, and in this style the hill was mounted, only to disappoint us, as from horizon to horizon was seen only one dense sea of scrub.

The sight of the pair of us was as ludicrous as distressing; myself plodding along first, through mud and water, attired only in a Crimean shirt, hair unkempt and streaming in the wind, with over a week's stubble on my chin; cheeks hollow with hunger and hardship; with the strap over one shoulder pulling up my wife, who was in as forlorn a condition as myself—her hat gone, boots worked into a pulp, dress clinging to her, bespattered with mud till her own mother would not have known her. At this point she completely gave in and lay on the ground quite exhausted.

After a consultation we decided that I should follow the track, in the hope of finding some place of refuge; and promising to return in an hour, I started off at a double quick, hoping to cover more space in my hour by running. Having travelled some two miles I was rejoiced to see a mob of working bullocks and horses having bells on them, which plainly told me that a teamsters' camp was not far from us.

The apparition of so strange a looking object as myself startled the cattle, and they scampered off, their bells wildly sounding through the stillness of the bush. I determined to follow this team, no matter where they went, and I kept close to their heels over hill and dale, and was soon repaid by coming up to a camp of bullock drivers, who turned out bewildered at the unusual sight, concluding I was a madman. It took me some time to convey to them our situation, and they always affirmed I was light-headed when I arrived at their camp; for I told them, among other things, that we were all drowned, when they replied that they thought me a pretty lively specimen of a drowned man.

My first thought was to return to my wife, but these rough sons of the forest suggested that some clothing would be an improvement to me, so one produced a pair of moleskin trousers, another a sou'-wester, while a third found a pair of boots. These articles of civilization revealed to me my condition; my legs had been wounded, probably by snags in the river, and my feet were so cut and swollen that boots were simply instruments of torture.

My new acquaintances bewailed the low state of their larder, consisting of one damper (a kind of thick pancake), with no hope of getting more provisions till the flood went down. A slice of this bush fare was handed me, part of which I devoured, and hoarded up the rest for my better half. The men now saddled three horses, and I mounted one, leading another for my wife, and one of the men accompanied me. We started in quest of the lost one.

The search proved a difficult task, as I had left the road when following the cattle, and all the country was strange to me. We ultimately reached the spot, to find her gone. We discovered her, however, further along the road. It appears she fell asleep, and her mind evidently wandered, for, upon awaking, she fancied numerous black stumps were wild natives; and in her fear she ran down the road. The sight of a company of horsemen also frightened her, as she failed to recognize her husband in his new attire. Fortunately my Crimean shirt attracted her attention, so, despite sou'-wester and moleskins, she acknowledged her chief. It was a mixture of pain and amusement to see her tackle the damper, dry and tasteless as it was; but after twenty-four hours' starvation and hardship in the open air, her appetite was considerably sharpened, till the coarsest food was a luxury.

We now returned to the camp, where we found four drays loaded with wool. The men usually slept under these drays, and one dray was given up to us. The first work was to gather long grass to make a bed, and an old blanket was supplied us, and we felt happy at the perfect rest we enjoyed. To bathe and dress my wounds took some time, and a good sleep made a wonderful improvement in us. We found we were in a bend of the river Mackenzie, and shut off from the rest of the world by this swollen torrent. Nine days were spent in watching the river subside. During this time our fare was scanty and uncertain. Occasionally a parrot was shot, which made good stew, but maize (carried as horse feed) was our main stay. This we boiled, and became heartily sick of it before our nine days' imprisonment were over.

One thought haunted me: What has become of my brother? After seven days' waiting, we rode on horseback some twelve miles to where a public-house was built on the opposite bank. The river had now retired to its natural channel, and, by shouting across, communication was opened up with this grog shanty. I ascertained that a man answering the description of my brother had been found by some stock-riders, and he was now at Columbra station. After much persuasion I got a man to ride over and inform him of our safety, and of my desire to see him, and appointed this spot for the meeting place next day. Sharp to the minute we met, he on one side of the river and I on the other, and as he recognized me he threw up his hat and gave a lusty hurrah!

It was now arranged that he should ride to our station, Oakey Creek, about thirty miles distant, and get horses for us, as we hoped to cross in a day or two. This he did, and returned next day with the station manager, and several men with axes, for the purpose of making a canoe out of a gum tree, to ferry us across. They set to work with a will, and two days were occupied in felling a large tree, and hollowing a canoe from its trunk. This tedious work proved a failure, as the tree being green, was not sufficiently buoyant; empty kegs were resorted to to make the craft more seaworthy, and after weary watching we saw my brother and the manager steer for our side, but, alas for all things human! the middle of the stream was not reached when a sunken snag was struck, and over went the boat and occupants, both of whom were seen floundering in the water. A few minutes of suspense and they were seen nearing the bank they left, and were soon safely landed. Our friends, the bullock drivers, now ferried us across in a bark canoe.

We were rather shy of so frail a craft after our recent experience, but the river was now comparatively small, and no alternative offered. We now repaired to the grog shanty and had what we considered a sumptuous repast, consisting of salt junk and pumpkin, and a monster plum pudding. After this we mounted our steeds and rode thirty miles

SETTLER'S HOME.

"Far in the wilderness obscure
　The lonely mansion lay,
A refuge to the neighboring poor,
　And strangers led astray.

"No stores beneath its humble thatch
　Required anxious care;
The wicket opening with a latch
　Received the loving pair."

home. Considering my wife had been half-starved for a fortnight, and exposed to all the vicissitudes before related, a ride of thirty miles without a rest, shows what a Victorian native can do. Such is the experience we passed through, and we now record our thanks to Almighty God for having almost miraculously rescued us from a watery grave, in the first instance, and secondly, by saving us from a worse fate of being lost in the Queensland bush.

Many months afterwards, when the river was dried to a chain of water-holes, we visited the scene of our peril, and found the tree upon which we clung all night; the bough upon which we stood showed there had been thirty feet of water under us when we swam for our lives. We took a plank from the tree, which has been made into a casket bearing a silver plate giving its history, which we leave to our children as a memento of our perilous adventure on April 1st, 1869.

MR. SAMUEL BARBER'S DESCRIPTION.

It was on the 1st day of April, 1869, a fine morning, although at times cloudy. Our breakfast was none of the best, as our rations were running short, but being full of hope and youthful vigor, we were quite ready when the canoe was finished to make the attempt to cross the river. My brother had a small life-belt which we both thought he had better put on—he being a married man—and after loading the canoe with a portmanteau containing my sister-in-law's linen, and also some small jewellery, such as rings, brooches, etc., we put off, and without mishap reached, as we thought, the opposite shore.

Having landed and discharged cargo, my brother returned for his wife. I could see them plainly, and all went well till they got into the middle of the current when, for some cause or other, the canoe appeared to become unmanageable, and began to go round and round, so much so that I became alarmed, and leaving the portmanteau ran along the bank so as to keep up with them (as they drifted with the current) and render assistance if possible. Having run some fifty yards I found, to my dismay, that I could get no further, being cut off by a strong current coming from the westward, which I afterwards found was the Mackenzie.

As the canoe and its occupants were, by this time, out of sight, I began to fear for my own safety, for with a little exploring I soon realized the fact that I was on an island, the highest part of which was not more than a foot above the water, the long grass, which was four or five feet high, having deceived us as to the real character of the ground. As night was coming on, and I hoped my brother would come with the canoe in the morning to rescue me, I thought I would make myself as comfortable as circumstances permitted for the night, so having selected the tree on the highest ground, and strapping the portmanteau on my back, I climbed up, and on reaching a pair of forked branches about fifteen feet up, pressed the portmanteau tightly down and sat on it. Having attained this comfortable position, a thunderstorm broke overhead and the rain came down in torrents, making me considerably damp.

However, it did not last long, for by nine o'clock the stars shone out, and I rejoiced to hear my brother and sister-in-law singing hymns. I was very glad of this and thought they could not be so badly off, and that now I was pretty sure of being rescued in the morning, so I coo-eed (called) a good many times, but it did not seem to have much effect, as they still went on singing.

I didn't have a very lively time of it, and was afraid to go to sleep for fear of falling off the roost, so was glad when the morning began to dawn. When daylight appeared, however, my island was gone—clean disappeared, and a strong current was running at the foot of my tree. Not a sign of grass or anything remained to show that an island existed overnight. The bank of the river that I wanted to gain was in sight, but at a considerable distance, and divided from me by a surging current.

I still hoped that my brother would come, and soon heard his voice much nearer than it sounded overnight, so I shouted at the top of my voice that I was on an island and flooded, and asked him to come and take me off; but the birds were singing so joyously in the morning sunshine, the laughing jackasses near me keeping up a continuous peal of laughter, as if they thought my presence amongst them was a huge joke, that gradually my brother's voice died away and I heard it no more.

Having waited till ten o'clock, by which time I had probably been in the tree for thirteen or fourteen hours, and a long time having now elapsed since my brother had gone, I began to fear that something must have happened to them, and perhaps their lives were in danger, or that they had been unable to save themselves.

With this idea I made up my mind to swim for the shore, and began to divest myself of my clothes. It was a helmet hat that I wore, and for the sake of ventilation there was an aperture round my head. In putting my watch inside my hat, I found there three scorpions and two large centipedes, which had taken refuge there and seemed quite happy and contented, having been, like myself, hunted up the tree by the water. I realized a kind of " fellow feeling" for them; however, I shook them out, and falling into the water they went down with the current. Having fixed my watch in their place I began to slip down the tree.

I did not feel in very good spirits, being cold and hungry and alone, and slipping down a tree with rough bark, without nether garments on, isn't nice; besides I was afraid the water might be cold and give me the cramp. I had to go, however, and what was my joy when I found the river literally a warm bath and was so comforting and exhilarating that I never felt more able to swim than at that time.

My clothes had been rolled into a small bundle, with a string attached, which I took in my teeth. It was about waist deep at the foot of the tree, so having got a good start, I made for the shore. After going a good long way a log came past, which I thought a good opportunity of resting on, but it would bear no weight, and in getting over it my bundle got entangled, and I had to swim and get it free, but at last had the satisfaction of gaining the bank safely, and walking up on to dry land. Having wrung out my clothes and dressed, I began to wonder what I would do next.

Having heard that there was a bridle track near

this spot to Columbra station, which was used by the mail-man, I determined to try and find it, but after hunting a long while had to give it up, and then having a pocket compass, I struck out towards the west, having heard that this was the direction of the station. About mid-day I came to some scrub so dense that it presented an impenetrable barrier, for the saplings were so close as to make it impossible to get through them.

I then thought I would climb a tree, and soon came to a regular giant, with a smaller one growing close to it; the latter I climbed, and from its top branches got into the limbs of its taller brother, and by this means got up to the very top branches, in the hope that some signs of the station or other habitation might be visible.

In this I was again disappointed, for the tops of the trees, as far as my eyes could reach, formed an apparent even surface like the sea. I now began to give up hope, but I thought it would be better to go back to the river, as there would at least be water to drink, which might sustain life till succour came, for there was still a lingering hope that my brother might come to my rescue.

On my way back to the river I must have struck more to my right hand than I intended, for suddenly, on a small stony ridge, I crossed a track, which instinct told me was the very one desired, and so certain was I, that with renewed vigor I went along till my spirits received a damper by finding that it ran across some flooded gullies. Possibly by going a long round these gullies might have been "headed," but in the fear that if once lost the track might not again be found, I took off my clothes and swam over, striking the track on the other side, and after wringing out my clothes and dressing, my journey was resumed.

This swimming of creeks and gullies had to be done two or three times, and then the track left the low ground, and the travelling became easier. A new trouble now assailed me, the track became so overgrown with grass that I lost it many times, and believing that my only chance lay in following it, I crept on my hands and knees, parting the grass and feeling for the horses' tracks. Even this plan failed at last, and about sundown it became cloudy and began to rain.

In despair I lay down under a bush, and, being very faint and tired from long travelling and hunger, fell into a kind of doze, from which I was suddenly awakened by the report of a stock whip.

Jumping up, I ran in the direction the sound came from, and was rejoiced to see two men driving a mob of cattle. As I called loudly to them, they soon saw me, and one of them came over to me, thinking that I must be a wandering madman, as he thought no sane traveller could be in that neighborhood, owing to the state of the rivers.

In a few hurried words I explained how it was that I came to be there, and he advised me to follow him and his companion who were going to Columbra with the cattle, one of which they were going to kill for beef. Being within two miles of the station, I was soon there, and was most kindly received by the manager's wife, Mrs. McLennan, who speedily set some food before me. As night closed in, the rain came down again in torrents, and as I lay awake hearing it pattering on the roof, I thought of my brother and his wife, and wondered whether they had found shelter or not.

I knew that Joss's station was down the river from where we crossed, and believed they might have gone there, but the enormous body of water in the river made it next to impossible for us to find out for a certainty.

On the fourth day of my stay at Columbra a man came from a public-house situated on the bank of the Mackenzie, about three miles further up than Columbra (which was away back, and not in sight of the river), with a message to the effect that my brother and sister-in-law had fallen in with some teams that were camped on the other side of the river, and that he desired to see me next morning. This was good news indeed, and sharp at the appointed time I went and was rejoiced to see him safe and well, and to hear that his wife was at their camp, bravely bearing her misfortunes.

After a good many explanations on both sides, and congratulations at all our lives having been spared, we began to speak of getting him and his wife over the river, which was still very high, and the distance between us made it very difficult to carry on conversation.

I told him that the mail-man (who was weather-bound) and the stockman had offered to go with me to the junction of the rivers where we tried to cross, and swim over to the island so as to get the portmanteau from the tree, as the contents would by that time have received damage from wet. He was glad to hear this, and said he would go to the river just above the junction, and we might meet him there and shout across the river the news as to how we succeeded. Accordingly, next day the two men before mentioned and myself rode to the Isaacs river and, after tying our horses up (excepting one, which we took with us) swam over to the island. It was with different feelings that I now breasted the current to return to the island to those experienced on leaving it, and it now was just a mud bank, looking very desolate and dirty. We soon espied the portmanteau high up in the tree, and this time the mail-man went up, and we soon had it down. Then, strapping it on the horse, we made him swim back to his companions, ourselves following.

Having dressed, and mounted our steeds, we ran the river Mackenzie, up to where we expected to see my brother. He was already there, and was glad to hear of the safety of his wife's portmanteau and its contents.

Having told me to proceed on the morrow to our station (Oakey Creek), a distance of thirty-four miles from Columbra, and bring back a buggy or express waggon in which he and his wife might go home as soon as they could cross the river, we bade each other good-bye, and while he returned to his camp, I and my companion returned to Columbra, and my kind hostess took the things (which sadly needed attending to) from the portmanteau.

Next day, with a borrowed horse, I started for Oakey Creek, and excepting that the horse gave out when about two-thirds over the journey, and having to swim a creek on his back, which wet me nearly up to my neck, and having to walk the last few miles and drive the horse with a stick in front, nothing happened to mar the enjoyment of my journey, so that about sunset I got to Oakey Creek station. Mr. Macfarlane, the manager, lent me some clothes, mine being wet and bedrabbled, and having heard of our misfortunes, decided to return next morning with me, and take an overseer with him and also some tools, that we might make a canoe in order to rescue my friends.

We put up at the public-house on the banks of the river, and for three days worked terribly hard to make a canoe; Mr. Macfarlane thought we had better fell a gum tree and scoop it out in preference to making a canoe of bark. I had my doubts as to the wisdom of this, but being a much younger man, gave in, and we set to work. The wood being green and full of sap we procured some empty brandy kegs from the public-house and lashed two on either side of the canoe to render it more buoyant.

One keg (the fifth) had one end gone and thinking it a pity to lose the aid of this one, I suggested lashing it with its open end up at the stern, and this we did.

When we were putting the finishing touches to the canoe, my brother, who was getting very impatient, came and sat on the bank on the opposite side of the river and wanted to know when we were going to launch it, and remarked that the men with him were making a bark canoe, and said further that if we did not look smart their canoe would be ready first. We said he had better wait for ours and promised that it should be ready the next morning.

Having got our ship into the water we prepared to embark. Mr. Macfarlane advised taking off our boots, as he said "something might happen." We then began to run down with the current, intending to go to a place where the absence of trees would make it less dangerous to cross.

Soon after starting we were surprised to see my brother on the side we had just left, and asked him how he got there. He told us that the men with him had finished their canoe, and being tired of waiting he had got one of them to put him over. He asked us whether our canoe was seaworthy, and began to make joking remarks about it—thought it was a "rakish-looking craft," and wondered what we carried in "that thing" at the stern. We told him that was the place where we carried the mail.

Jokes and good humor prevailed for a short time, when right at our bows was a huge limb of a tree, which, although broken down, still hung to the tree, while its small branches were in the water, and kept swaying to and fro with the force of the current. Into this we went with a smash, and in a second the canoe was overturned and I found myself clinging to this limb. Notwithstanding the weight of the current pressing on my chest, which seemed as if it would tear my arms from their sockets, I could not make my hands let go their hold, and I can fully understand the clutch of a drowning man.

I looked for my companion and saw him fifty yards away clinging to the canoe. Just then he appeared to look for me, and shouted, "Come on, come on." With a great effort of will I managed to let go, to be immediately carried under water, but only for a few seconds.

On gaining the surface I struck out with might and main and, assisted by the current, made amazing headway so that the canoe was soon overtaken, although the effort somewhat exhausted me.

Our gallant ship now floated level with the water and threatened to go down altogether, so we had to content ourselves with clinging to it, and by kicking against all the trees we passed, we gradually worked it to the shore.

All this time my brother was running along the river bank, blowing up his life-belt (which he managed to retain all through his troubles), thinking he might have to go in and try to save one or other of us. My hat and Mr. Macfarlane's waistcoat were floating on the stream about one hundred yards down, so my brother said, "Here, put this belt on and get your hat." "No fear," said I; "I'm not going in there any more." "Why, you must have a hat," said he, and remembering the heat of the sun, I thought better of it, so hastily putting on the life-belt, ran along the river side till I got beyond the hat, and plunging in swam into the centre of the current and easily secured both articles as they came along.

It was rather disappointing to find that the little blocks that kept the ventilator in place, were gone: having been only glued in—so that the hat, under these circumstances, acted too much like an extinguisher, but it could not be helped, and having escaped with our lives amidst such danger made us look beyond such trifles as these. It need hardly be said that my brother determined to cross his wife over in the canoe in which he had come, so that while Mr. Macfarlane and I went back to the public-house to change our clothes, he returned to her and said he thought she had better come over in the bark canoe, stating (and possibly with a good deal of truth) that it was the better of the two. In a short time she was safely ferried across, and as they walked up to the hotel she was told of our mishap.

It was a pleasant thing to be all together again after such a chapter of accidents, and I am sure we all felt truly thankful to the Giver of all good things that our lives had been spared amidst such dangers.

Having had some dinner, the horses were saddled, and, some hours after dark, we reached our destination in safety.

AUSTRALIA AND HOMEWARD;

OR,

MELBOURNE TO LONDON.

INTRODUCTORY NOTE.

IN 1886 I was delegated by the Dominion Alliance to represent Canada at the British and Colonial Temperance Congress appointed to be held in London, England, in July of that year, at the time of the Colonial and Indian Exhibition.

While speaking at that Congress I became acquainted with several Australians, who invited me to come to Australia and deliver addresses on the subject of Temperance, under the auspices of the Victorian Temperance Alliance.

The gentlemen referred to were Mr. J. W. Hunt, Chairman of the Executive Committee, and Messrs. Samuel Rudduck and William Hutchinson, members of the Alliance.

After receiving a cablegram from Melbourne to the effect that the Committee had sanctioned the suggestion made by these gentlemen, my wife and I left Montreal for Melbourne on the 23rd day of January, and arrived at our destination, after a very pleasant voyage, on the 17th of March, 1887.

The letters which follow are reproduced from the *Christian Guardian*, to which they were written during our voyage "Homeward."

D. V. L.

Australia and Homeward;

OR,

MELBOURNE TO LONDON.

FIRST LETTER.

ON the evening of the 14th of December, 1887, a gathering of near 2,000 of the Melbourne temperance people was held in the City Hall to give us a farewell, and to celebrate a Local Option victory, which the friends of temperance had just secured in the Victorian Legislature. The Hon. James Munro, the President of the Victorian Alliance, presided. The Hon. J. B. Patterson and the Hon. J. Balfour, C. J. Ham, M.P., J. Russell, M.P., as also several ministers of various denominations, took part, among them that giant preacher and temperance worker, the Rev. A. R. Edgar (Wesleyan), whom everybody, except the publican, loves. The chairman, in his opening address, was kind enough to refer to my work as having given satisfaction to the Alliance. Mr. J. W. Hunt, whom I met in London in 1886, and who afterwards called to see me in Montreal in regard to my coming to Australia, presented me with an address in the name of the Alliance. The newspaper reporter says of it: "The address, expressive of the high esteem in which he and Mrs. Lucas are held, and of the good wishes for their future welfare, is richly illuminated and handsomely bound in morocco, forming a work of art of which the recipient might well be proud." If I may be proud of the artistic get-up of the address, I should have a strange heart indeed if I were not very much more proud, or at any rate thankful, for what it contains. Never, in all my life, have I been more conscious of the Divine favor; never more fully convinced that I was working for God and humanity. Counting sermons and other talks on the Sabbath, I have spoken, on the average, eight times a week for the past six months. Sometimes I have spoken eleven times a week. During the whole campaign not one appointment was missed. All thanks be to God.

A copy of the Address will be found on the opposite page.

ADDRESS

TO THE REV. D. V. LUCAS, M.A., OF CANADA.

Dear Sir,—

The Committee of the Victorian Alliance, together with the members and friends of this and kindred associations, upon the occasion of your departure from their midst, at the close of your mission in Victoria in furtherance of the cause of Local Option, desire to assure you of their gratification at your visit, to testify to the good accomplished thereby, and to express their sincere wishes for your future welfare.

In the course of your work throughout the colony you have won the esteem and admiration of those with whom you have been brought in contact, and numerous testimonies have been received as to the good accomplished by your labors in helping to bring the Local Option question to a successful issue.

It is desired to include in this tribute of respect and admiration your partner in life, who has ably seconded your efforts by her work for Temperance amongst the women of Victoria.

Should you be enabled to return to this colony, you may rest assured that you would receive a hearty welcome from those amongst whom you have labored during your present visit.

In bidding you farewell, the hope is cherished that you and your dear wife may long be spared to fight the good fight for Temperance, and, under the Divine blessing, with ever-increasing success.

     JAMES MUNRO, *President, V.A.*
     J. W. HUNT, *Chairman,* "
     J. W. MEADEN, *Hon. Sec'y,* "
     DAVID BEATH, *Treasurer,* "
     JOHN VALE, *Secretary,* "

We left Melbourne early Thursday morning, Dec. 15th. We reached Ararat about 2 p.m.; wife went on to Stawell, while I took a branch line for Hamilton, where I was to deliver a farewell lecture, having been advertised so to do in the Hamilton *Spectator*. Returned next day to Ararat, which has a lofty and beautiful mountain near by, at the foot of which rests an ark of refuge, in the form of a capacious and handsomely built benevolent asylum. The region round about Ararat is among the pretty portions of the colony of Victoria.

Having lectured at Stawell, we left by the midnight express for Adelaide, which is distant from Melbourne five hundred miles west by rail. Sydney is about the same distance from Melbourne, but in the opposite direction. We spent a very pleasant fortnight at Adelaide, the capital of South Australia.

We visited the Industrial Exhibition, which may be regarded as very creditable for a colony founded just fifty years ago. Adelaide is much more beautiful than Melbourne as regards natural scenery. The city is almost completely surrounded by lovely and picturesque hills. We were there on Christmas, and had, at a Christmas family dinner to which we were kindly invited, ripe figs, strawberries, apricots, cherries and plums, all just fresh from the garden.

Christmas with the thermometer at 95° in the shade was quite a new experience. Although anything may seem all right when we get used to it, yet it seems to me nothing could ever reconcile me to 95° above zero at Christmas times. To crown all, I saw in the windows of the shops here old Santa Claus clad in his sheepskin, long-woolled coat. Such contradictions as there are in this world any way! The old chap did not appear to look anything like so happy as we have seen him in the pictures, with his reindeer and his sledge and robes, down in the street, while he is on the roof in the light of the moon fighting with the cats for the right of way down the chimney. Shortly after reaching Adelaide I received a note from a gentleman whom I met in Montreal four years ago, T. O.

Jones, Esq., formerly Mayor of Gawlor (the second in size among the cities of South Australia), inviting us out to visit him.

Mr. Jones has a sister in Montreal and a daughter in Winnipeg, so, of course, he feels strongly attached to Canada. Having travelled over most of the Dominion, he is thoroughly conversant with all things Canadian, so it was like meeting one "to the manor born" to meet him, and we had, during the short time at our command, a very pleasant time of it. There was a Christmas Sabbath-school gathering in the Town Hall. I had the honor of giving an address to parents and children, nearly two thousand in all.

We left Adelaide on the afternoon of December 31st, by the steamship *Massilia*, of the Peninsular and Oriental Line, and were quite out of sight of land before the end of the old year. The day which has always been to me a day of gladness, was made a day of sorrow through the painful death of one of our passengers. A young man, twenty-six years of age, came on at Melbourne, suffering with *delirium tremens*. He became so unmanageable on Saturday night that the stewards had to bind him down, hands and feet. O, what a comment on the crying out of our opponents for liberty!

In Melbourne a party was formed to oppose us,

called "The Liberty of the Subject Defence League." That the subject's liberty may be perpetuated let this young man be bound. What though he be a graduate with honors from one of the greatest of the universities. The same has occurred before; let him be bound. What though he is one of the kindest-hearted men when sober, and of a most pleasant disposition, he must now be bound, lest in his mad moments he might kill some one; or, as the captain said to me, he might jump overboard and be the means of drowning some of the seamen trying to save him, and he must be bound. Poor fellow; see him struggle! That liberty, poor boy, for which your slaughterers contend, often comes to this. O, Liberty, what chains are sometimes forged in thy name!

How many such poor fellows are bound in even worse than hard cord and iron chains, that brewers, distillers and publicans may have the liberty to slaughter. But our poor fellow-traveller has given up the struggle; he is quiet now. How pale he is! O God! he is dead! Dead, just as the Sabbath New Year morn is ushered in. O, what a beginning for the new year! And now there is but one thing more we can do for him; wind him up and commit him to the deep. Our hearts go out in sadness towards the poor mother in the old land, who will go down to her grave mourning when she learns the fate of her child. We must not content ourselves with weeping with those who weep for their slain.

We can never rest while this foul blot remains upon the fair face of our Christianity: while this loathsome excrescence, the liquor traffic, deforms the stature of civilization.

After leaving Adelaide we were a little over three days in crossing the "Great Australian Bight." I suppose most readers will understand better if I call it a bay. I presume navigators or geographers regard it as too big for a bay, or too much open to the sea, so "bight" is the word, where bay or sound would have been more familiar. Think of it as a well-bent bow. We sail along the string a little over one thousand miles.

Having left Adelaide on Saturday evening, we steam into King George's Sound, and anchor off the pretty little city of Albany, at 10 p.m. Tuesday. Like the harbor at Sydney (Port Jackson), this is a beautiful harbor. Not so much so as the former, but sufficiently so as to be classed with it, and, like Port Jackson, can be made, without large outlay, almost as impregnable as Gibraltar. I was surprised to find that our ship of five thousand tons could anchor so close to the town.

A wharf is now being constructed which, in a very

short time, will enable all ships to dispense with the use of a lighter. Railroads are being built; one along the west coast to Perth, and another is being pushed forward in the direction of Adelaide. When that is completed, the Australians will then have a transcontinental system. I have not been able to learn much of the vast country lying between King George's Sound and Adelaide.

If there is good soil, no doubt there will, ere long, be rapid immigration, especially if these roads should soon be completed. The greatest lack with Australia is water. There is an abundance of good soil, which is almost valueless from the want of this very necessary element. Of late, in some parts, abundant water has been obtained by boring. Rains are so unreliable, the mainstay of the agriculturist, and more especially the fruit-grower or gardener, is irrigation. So whether the western part of the continent will be settled up rapidly or not all depends.

INDIAN OCEAN, *January 6th, 1888.*

SECOND LETTER.

WE steamed out of King George's Sound on Wednesday, 4th January, at 6 a.m. We are having the most pleasant voyage I have ever experienced. The wind is most favorable to our progress. We ran into the tropics on Saturday, and so are pretty certain to have it warm for the next fortnight, especially as we have to cross the equator.

You will form some idea of our ship when I say that it requires a crew, all told, of 187 to man her, from the captain down to the bootblack. Our doctor is the son of our distinguished fellow-Canadian, Sir William Dawson, of Montreal. If the son should turn out to be as good a man as his father, it will always be considered an honor to have known him. Part of our crew is made up of Africans and Mohammedans.

We were greatly amused to see these fellows taking their meal, which consists largely of rice, with curry or gravy. They sit down upon the deck around a dish. One pours in the gravy, when each with his right hand mixes up from the pile before them a ball, half the size of his fist, and puts it in

". . . . The sea being smooth
How many shallow bauble boats dare sail
Upon her patient breast, making their way
With those of nobler bulk!
But let the ruffian Boreas once enrage
The gentle Thetis, and anon behold
The strong-ribb'd bark through liquid mountains cut,
Bounding between the two moist elements
Like Perseus' horse. Where's then the saucy boat
Whose weak untimber'd sides but even now
Co-rival'd greatness? Either to harbor fled
Or made a toast for Neptune."
—*Shakespeare.*

his mouth, and then proceeds to mix up another, all eating from the same dish. Only the right hand is used in conveying food to the mouth.

They have with them a priest, or at least one who does the work of a priest, and Mohammedan prayers are read in the forecastle each evening at sundown.

READING THE KORAN.

I understand that one reason why the company employ these men is because they are all, by their religion, pledged teetotallers, and never give the officers of the ship any trouble by those undisciplinary pranks which usually grow out of grog-drinking.

They have among them "headmen," or bosses, who

have chains about their necks to which whistles are attached; and when one of these barefooted officials has occasion to pipe up his men to lower or put up a sail, he makes you feel the exalted dignity of his position by the sublime way in which he blows his whistle. If you are reading or writing or conversing, you are often made to experience, with Dr. Franklin, that "you have to pay dear for the whistle."

Our watches at sea, as we pass from one degree of longitude to another, are something like the clock of that man who said of it, that when the hour hand was at nine, and the minute hand at eleven, and it struck four, then he knew it was exactly half-past three. It is useless to try to set them right, when we are steering east or west. One must learn to trust entirely to the ship's bells, which toll out in half-hour strokes the progress of the watches into which the day and night are divided.

Through the night it is pleasant to hear the men on the watch cry out and respond to each other. I suppose the rule is so made that the officer in command, through that watch, may know that his men are awake and on the look-out. When the bell strikes, the watchman on the main bridge cries out in a kind of chant, "Ky-ah dek-tah hai?"—(What do you see?) The man on the forward bridge responds, in a long drawn-out note, "Kootchnai,"—(I see nothing). Then the quartermaster, also on the forward bridge, in English, with a fuller, rounder and louder key, announces that "All's well!"—and so on, at every half-hour of the night, if you should happen to be awake, you may know that faithful men are at their posts, guiding your ship through the darkness on her way to your desired haven.

What small events relieve the monotony of a landsman's life at sea. To meet a ship is a wonderful sight after looking for a week or a fortnight at the wide waste of waters: a whale, a school of porpoises, a whole flock of flying-fish, startled into the air by the rude intrusion of our huge leviathan, ploughing *sans ceremonie* right in among them. Sometimes these little creatures, when once out of the water, will fly straight for the lights of the ship.

One came on board a few evenings ago. It fell on the deck, and one of the stewards brought it into the dining-saloon for us to look at. I have seen them in thousands in various parts of the Pacific Ocean, but never thought them so large. This one was quite a foot in length, and would weigh not less than a pound. Its wings were about half the size of a lady's fan.

Well, well, what next? Here's something more exciting. All's well that ends well, and so, I suppose, we can afford to be jocular over what might have been serious. If fishes jump into the ship, men, to be even with them, sometimes jump into the sea. "Man overboard!" All hands rush to the deck. The ship is stopped, engines reversed, buoys thrown out, boats lowered. "Pull away, boys, to the eastward, half a mile astern: follow the track of the ship."

Fortunately it is a lovely morning. There is just enough swell to give a graceful motion to the boat gone out in search. All opera-glasses are in requisition; all eyes scan the surface of the water. "There he is! See, the boat is pulling straight for him." Five minutes later up goes an oar, like a mast to the boat, a signal that they have him. When he is safe on board again, we can ask, Who is he? and how came he off the ship?

"So ho, my lad, so ho!" One of the African black fellows, who has given the officers a good deal of trouble before, now, rather than work, plays "sick." When the doctor reports that he can find nothing the matter with him, he is ordered by the boss with the whistle to go to work: and, in a fit of passion, he pops over.

However, a man in new circumstances and cold water sometimes changes his mind, and my jolly tar no sooner reaches the surface, after his plunge, than he wishes himself back on the ship. When the boat gets near him he is shouting like a good fellow, and swimming for dear life. He now weareth a chain. When we reach Colombo (Ceylon) he will be relieved from the difficulties and dangers of the ocean and allowed to do a little work for the benefit of the State and for his board—simply to teach him that insubordination at sea is a game which cannot be played with impunity.

We have just crossed the equator for the second time, having crossed it about nine thousand miles east of this point in March last. We are once more in the Northern Hemisphere. We are having very pleasant weather. Temperature, 82°.

INDIAN OCEAN, *January 14th, 1888.*

THIRD LETTER.

THE last letter was written just before we reached Ceylon. We dropped anchor in Colombo harbor at 4 a.m. Sunday, 15th January. Colombo is a city of 120,000 inhabitants, of these about 2,000 are English-speaking. I preached in the evening in the "oldest Wesleyan chapel in Asia." It was built in 1816. It is well situated as respects population, being in one of the crowded parts of the city. It contained a large marble tablet, erected to the memory of the great and good Dr. Coke. May 3rd, 1814, that good man ascended to his reward.

The tablet tells us that his body was buried at sea, lat. 2.29 south, long. 59.29 west. It also bears the name of those honored brethren who accompanied him in his glorious work. The names are Lynch, Squance, Harvard, Erskine and Clough.

Although the good Coke never reached the shore towards which his heart and his prayers went out, I presume the work would not have been begun, at any rate so soon as it was, if he had not led the way. When the sea shall give up her dead, what a great host will stand upon these shores to hail the resurrection of this zealous servant and apostle of God!

DATE PALMS.

I was very much pleased with the singing and apparent devotion of the native people. One could not fail to see the wonderful difference which a pure, experimental Christianity effects between those who embrace it and those who retain the belief in and practice of other forms of religion. There may be said to be five forms of religion in Ceylon—Protestantism, Roman Catholicism, Buddhism, Hindooism and Mohammedanism.

Ceylon may be regarded as the chief centre of Buddhism. It began in India, but took refuge, after suffering terrible persecutions from the Brahmins, in this very lovely and very historic island. When the Emperor Ming of China had dreamed of seeing a golden man flying about his palace, and the dream was interpreted to mean that the Holy One was to be found in the West, having heard (as I think) a description of Jesus and His wonderful words and works, he despatched a deputation westward in search of the Holy One.

This deputation returned, after many months, with priests and images of Buddha from Ceylon. So going out from this island, that system has long been the widespread religion of China. Of the two, as a merciful and equalizing system Buddhism is very much superior to Brahminism.

There is a grand Buddhist temple in Colombo. There are a little over 1,500,000 Buddhists; Hindoos, 600,000; Roman Catholic, 200,000; Moham-

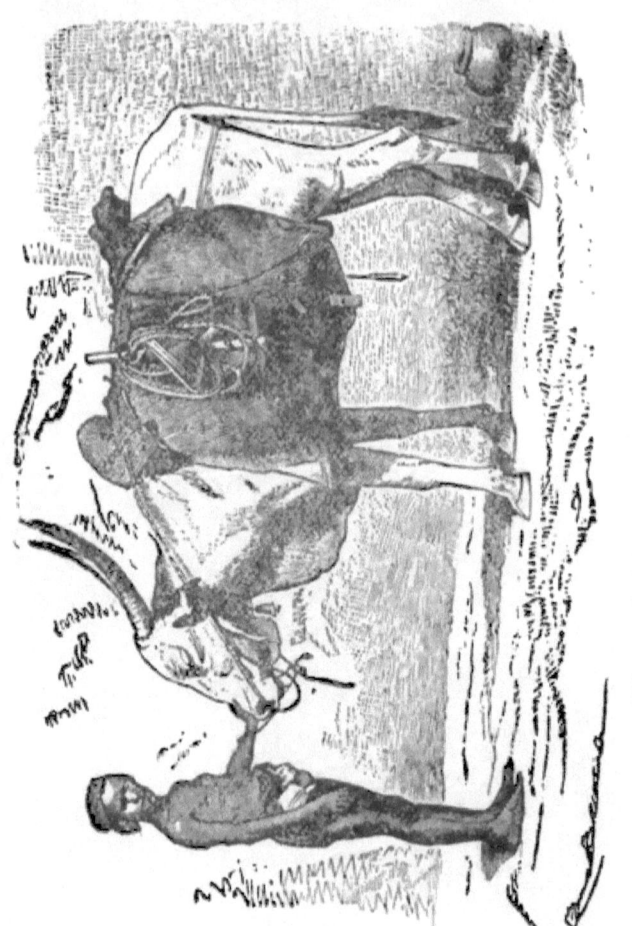

ONE MODE OF TRAVELLING IN CEYLON.

medans, 200,000; Protestants, somewhere under 100,000. There are in all about 23,000 Wesleyan adherents; of these about 5,000 are communicants. There are in round numbers 18,000 scholars in the Wesleyan schools.

ANOTHER MODE OF TRAVELLING IN CEYLON.

There is a Wesleyan College, over which the Rev. T. Moscrop presides, in which there are 300 pupils, 60 per cent. of whom are Christian. The Mohammedans who take advantage of the Wesleyan College attend the daily prayers with the others. Mr. Moscrop tells me, that although it is impossible to get the Mohammedans into any other place of worship (so called), yet they will listen with attention to what may be said upon the street. In a climate like that of Ceylon, out-door preaching might be the rule quite easily. Here is a glorious field for evangelistic work.

The Rev. John Scott is the Chairman of the Colombo District. He superintends the printing and publishing establishment. He kindly took me all through. Type-setting, printing, binding and stitching are all done by natives. I did not see among them all a white face. Books, leaflets, pamphlets, in the Singalese, are being prepared for scattering among the people, especially at promiscuous gatherings out of doors. I asked if they buy readily, or do they expect to receive them gratuitously. He says that the people buy very readily. Some of the Wesleyans are not only very devoted and exemplary, but are liberal givers.

I see, by referring to the report of the Colombo District, a copy of which Mr. Scott kindly gave me, that the number of conversions from Buddhism during the past year was fifty, and nine from Hindooism. The total number of pages of Scripture, religious and school books and tracts, printed in 1886, is 8,056,307. The report says that in the official list of publications issued by Government, the Wesleyan press continues to take the lead in vernacular literature. I had the good fortune to form the acquaintance of the Rev. S. Langdon, the Chairman of the Kandy District.

Mr. Langdon is doing a grand work in the interior. He is conducting his work more on the evangelistic principle. All these dear brethern seem to be men whose hearts are thoroughly in their work—a work which God is blessing. O that they may yet see still more abundant fruit of their labors.

Very nearly 3,000,000 of people in Ceylon; of these 275,000 are nominally Christian. Unfortunately a large number of those called Christians are hardly removed a hand-breadth above the Buddhist. If I were going to depend on mummery at all, I think I should choose the genuine Buddhistic article in preference to that called "Christian."

From what I saw for myself, and from the testimony of our brethren whose names I have given above, there are some in Ceylon called Christians who are so in more than name.

Mr. Scott gave me a wonderfully interesting account of the labors of one of their native preachers who won over to Christ six hundred of his countrymen, having to begin his work against the very strongest prejudices of the heathen people. There are now two large and prosperous circuits as the outcome of this good man's work, in addition to what he saw in his own day in this Eastern Hemisphere.

O, what a glorious field is here. Patient toilers have gone before in all these lands. They have opened the way. May we not enter into their labors with more of their zeal, that we may reap where they have sown, that by-and-bye, in the blessed harvest-home, the sowers and the reapers may rejoice together.

The first newspaper I got hold of had an article and a letter complaining of the increase of crime. I asked Mr. Scott if the increased use of intoxicants among the natives had anything to do with it, and his reply was that which we hear these times everywhere, viz., "Alcohol is the direct cause of more than half the crime known among us." This evil must be fought with greater earnestness. Of all the means the devil has ever invented for destroying the bodies and the souls of men, this is the most effective. These enemies and slaughterers of mankind—the makers and vendors of intoxicating beverages—must have no quarter. This is a holy war, and must be fought in the name of God.

There are many things more I wished to write about Ceylon, but must defer them. The sea to-day is as smooth as a floor. We have now come very nearly six thousand miles, and all the way we have had most delightful weather. I have written, all told, nearly two hundred pages of ordinary sized scribbling book.

INDIAN OCEAN, *January 18th, 1888.*

FOURTH LETTER.

THOUGH our ship is ploughing through the waves of the Arabian Sea, my thoughts go back to that island of spices which good Bishop Heber has set so many people singing about. I feel that there is very much more to be said about it than I have time to write now, or you have space to print. I said in my last letter that Ceylon may be regarded as the central point from which Buddhism has spread so largely over Asia. I believe it may be made the central point for the wider spread of Christianity.

Mr. Moscrop tells me that they are able to secure Christian teachers for all the children in their schools, which cannot be done in India. This is a most important feature, the percentage of conversion to Christianity of the better class of the people being much larger in Ceylon than on the continent of Asia.

The percentage of Christians to the whole population of the island is quite ten times that of India. Ceylon being the classic land of Buddhism, its downfall here would influence a vast proportion of the human race in Burmah, Siam and China. Arnold, in his "Light of Asia," gives us these lines:—

"We are the voices of the wandering wind,
  Which moan for rest, and rest can never find.
  Lo! as the wind is, so is mortal life,
  A moan, a sigh, a sob, a storm, a strife.

. . . .

"O Maya's son! because we roam the earth,
  Moan we upon these strings, we make no mirth;
  So many woes we see in many lands,
  So many streaming eyes and wringing hands.

. . . .

"But Thou that art to save, Thine hour is nigh!
  The sad world waileth in its misery,
  The blind world stumbleth on its round of pain.
  Rise, Maya's child! wake! slumber not again."

These lands must be filled with light. So far there are but faint rays. The sun is not yet fully risen, much less reached the meridian. We who know the truth may do much more than we are doing to roll this our poor earth with increasing speed towards the Sun of the soul.

Much might be done to spread the light by the formation of Christian bands for evangelistic tours round the world, for the purpose of strengthening the hands of pioneer brethren who sometimes grow weary in their heavy and responsible labors. How glad I shall be to join a company of earnest souls for such a work as this. O! let us hasten to "preach the Gospel to every creature." The time is short.

We look for a little at those factors which are at work in the direction of bringing Ceylon to Christ. The opening of the Suez Canal has tended to place her more in the centre of the ocean route through to the greater East. The English have constructed, at much expense, a breakwater which gives at Colombo a safe and capacious harbor.

Our ship added to her cargo at Colombo about three thousand tons, consisting partly of tea and coffee of Ceylon growth, and partly of raw silk brought down from China. By means of this increased trade Ceylon is brought more into contact with the Christian world, and is becoming every year more familiar with the British language and with Christian ideas.

So great was the value attached to this island as the "key of India," in addition to its natural wealth, that Britain at the general peace gave up, for its peaceable possession, the much larger island of Java to the Dutch. For about one hundred and fifty years the southern maritime districts of the island were occupied and controlled by the Portuguese, who were in 1656 driven out by the Dutch, who held them until the beginning of the present century, when the whole island came finally into the hands of the British Government, being converted into a Crown colony in 1803.

The army of Roman Catholic teachers brought in under Portuguese auspices had little difficulty in "converting" a good many thousands of a people who were only too ready to embrace a religion which gave them high-sounding baptismal names, and which in no sense prevented their continued observance of Buddhistic feasts and ceremonies. Besides, no appointments under the Government could be obtained without profession of Christian (R. C.) faith.

Little was done, therefore, by these teachers for the moral condition of the heathen, and very little was done by either the Portuguese or the Dutch to advance their material or intellectual condition. How great the contrast since the island came under British rule! In 1815 the total trade (exports and imports) was £473,000; in 1887 it was over £8,000,000. Shipping tonnage (entered and cleared), 75,000; in 1887 it was 4,000,000. In 1815 there were only 170 schools; now there are 2,200. Then there were 2,000 scholars; now there are 120,000.

Not only do we here see great material growth, but in this last item of statistics we see the present and future moral improvement of the people. One hundred and twenty thousand children in these schools, where every morning by governmental regulation the Bible is studied for one hour. Attendance during that hour is not compulsory, but pupils seldom or never absent themselves.

The present Governor, as most of his predecessors have done, takes a lively interest in the improvements of the country and its population. Mr. Langdon, Chairman of the Wesleyan Kandy District, tells me that the Governor feels a deep interest in his Christian work in the interior, and encourages it in every possible way.

The kings of Kandy were the last of all the native kings to hold out against the foreigners. There was a Kandyan tradition that their conquerors were to be a people who should make a road through the rocky hills. No one had attempted this until the British got possession of the country. The almost impenetrable interior has been opened up by the British. High hills were tunnelled for cart routes for the sake of getting at the valuable spices and other productions inland.

When the English landed, in 1796, there was not in the whole island a single practicable road. Before Sir E. Barnes resigned, in 1831, every town of importance was approached by a carriage road. He had constructed a first-class macadam road from Colombo to Kandy, which is now superseded by the railway of 1867.

By means of these roads not only have those in the heart of the country been materially benefited and more easily reached in times of famine, but by them also the Gospel, with its various means, is being very much more quickly and effectively brought to the people, fulfilling the words of Isaiah in his prophecies respecting the glorious and final ushering in of Gospel blessings to all people, "Prepare ye the way of the Lord, make straight in the desert a highway for our God. Every valley shall be exalted, and every mountain and hill shall be made low: and the crooked shall be made straight, and the rough places plain: and the glory of the Lord shall be revealed, and all flesh shall see it together: for the mouth of the Lord hath spoken it."

In 1807, the Governor's chaplain, writing to a friend in England, said: "Practically there are no roads in Ceylon." Now there are nearly 1,500 miles of metalled roads, besides 900 miles of gravelled, to which may be added 600 miles of improved sand roads available for traffic in dry weather.

The benefit to the people cannot be over-estimated. Waste districts have been settled up. Settlements, villages and towns have sprung up where fifty years ago all was jungle and desolation, and means of employment have been afforded the poor people. As in India, so it was in Ceylon in past ages; there was plenty of food in the country to feed the people, but in some districts they were dying by the thousand with famine, because there were no roads over which food could be conveyed in time. Now all this in Ceylon is changed.

An earnest writer has lately said that roads are great educators, and that especially in India and Ceylon, roads and railways are doing as much to level caste and destroy superstition as all the force of the missionaries and schoolmasters. Of this we may have our doubts, yet we rejoice in the hope that all these influences combine to bring about the dispersion of the darkness and the ushering in of the glorious day of truth. For this many prayers continually ascend.

ARABIAN SEA, *January 19th, 1888.*

FIFTH LETTER.

WE halted in the Arabian Sea, and put down a little babe to await the resurrection of the just, when the sea shall give up that vast host who rest beneath her troubled waves. I marked upon the map, in the pamphlet which the company give to the passengers, the latitude and longitude, for the poor mourning mother, that she might know the spot in the ocean where her little one sleeps its last sleep.

We passed on Saturday evening, 21st, Socotra Island, which the British Government has so lately taken, that, at least, other nations may be prevented from using it to the injury of British commerce, or to the weakening of the British hold upon the East. We passed Cape Guardafui about six o'clock on the Sabbath morning.

No light! That sharp point of land, extending well out into the sea, and no light to protect the sailor from wrecking his ship upon it! Why is there no light here, when all other such points that we have ever seen are well provided with these necessary beacons? Solely because if any nation were to put a lighthouse there it would have to maintain there, also, a garrison of soldiers to protect the lighthouse and its keeper from the savages. Alas, poor Africa! Thy coasts at every bay, or river, or anchorage, are stained with blood and tears. Poor Africa! Shall we wonder if thine hand is against the inventions of civilization! How much hast thou to thank civilization for?

All honor to those noble men, Livingstone and Stanley, and following them, Taylor and others, who have opened the way for better things, and are carrying in to our dark-skinned brethren the blessed light of truth and salvation.

Our supply of coal running short we had to put in to Aden, in Arabia, for a couple of hundred tons. This we had not expected. We anchored some little distance from the town, and the natives came out in hundreds, with all sorts of curios—chamois and gazelle horns, ostrich eggs, coral, white and pink; shells, fifty different kinds; walking sticks, native cloths, boxes, baskets, coral necklaces and so forth, and so forth.

We thought the natives of Colombo bad enough; but, O dear, as some said, they can't hold a candle to these fellows. "You buy, Mistuh! Me sell cheap.

Nice basket, Mistuh; lady want nice basket?" "Well, how much do you want for it?" "Two shillin', Mistuh; nice basket." "No, I don't want it. Take it away." "Mistuh, how much you give?" "No, take it away. I don't want it." "You give shillin', Mistuh?" "No. Take it away." "How much you give, Mistuh?" "Didn't I tell you, I don't want it? Take it away!" "How much you give, Mistuh? Say how much you give." "Well, look here, I'll give you sixpence for it." "Oh, Mistuh!" "I won't give you another penny for it. Take it away, and don't bother me." "All right, Mistuh. You take."

No sooner do the rest of the babbling crowd see you handing out money for a basket than down they rush on you like an avalanche, with all the above named articles and many more, with the same persistency and the same reduction and usually the same result. Like the girl who married her persistent admirer to get rid of him, so you buy things you don't want, just to get rid of these persevering traffickers. Now that we have bought till we positively affirm we will not buy any more, let us look down into the water.

O, shades of the vasty deep! what are those? Those, O vain man, those are your brethren. You thought that they were fish, porpoises, sharks, turtles, but they are not. They are your brethren, with just as good a right to be in that water as you have to be in this universe; with just as good a right to dive for sixpence as you have to dig for it.

"Trow away, Mistuh; me dive. You trow sixpence, Mistuh; you see me dive. Trow away, Mistuh; trow away! Yah, yah, yah! Ha, ha, ha!" O see his teeth! Who would begrudge a hundred pounds for such a set of teeth as that? "Trow away, Mistuh; you see me dive. Trow away! Yah, yah, yah! Ha, ha, ha!"

Now, my dear sir, you have been taught that "throwing money into the sea," is simply to waste it altogether, so that it does no one any good. Try it now, and see how some of your old notions are dissipated. You need not be very particular about tossing it quite close to him. Fifty or sixty feet from him or even more, so long as he can see where it strikes the water. Some one threw a sixpence right into the midst of a group of them, and four of them, reached it about the same time. They seized each other under the water, and we could see them in a regular quartette fight, heels uppermost, beneath the surface. When they came up the smallest one of the lot was crying. Whether he shed tears before he got to the surface or not I cannot say. I presume he could not very well answer that question himself. However, the biggest one had the money and the little one had the cry, and the intervening two had another turn at the "*Yah, yah, yah!* Ha, ha, ha Trow away, Mistuh; me dive."

Did I hear you ask about their clothing? A very insignificant matter, sir, very. The less said about it the better. Whether in or out of water, they thoroughly answer the conundrum which fond mothers so often put, "How shall we prevent our boys from wearing out the knees of their trousers?" Reduce them to the rank to which these fellows are reared, and send them forth "*sans culottes,*" and they give you no further trouble in this particular.

I am delighted to find that here at Aden a good work is being done in the distribution of Bibles, Testaments, and *portions* among the people. Only a short time ago there occurred the sound conversion of an Islam to the Christian faith. He has given himself up fully to colporteur and evangelistic work, and is already proving himself a workman that needeth not to be ashamed. Oh, how much these lands need a great army of such as he! May our God soon raise them up.

We weighed anchor at 4 p.m., and at ten o'clock

the same evening passed the narrow straits of Babel-mandeb, and entered the waters of the Red Sea, around which so many historic memories cling. The moon, nearly full, gives us a good view of the rocky coast and islands, for she is shining her very best, and is so directly above our heads that if the "man" were to fall off, he would drop squarely on our deck. And there, too, is our old friend the North Polar Star and the Dipper, with pointers well above the horizon at 11 p.m., with the handle still below the waves. We are reminded by the face of our old familiar friend that we are back again into the Northern Hemisphere, and begin already to have a home-like feeling.

A lady asked yesterday why the sea is called "Red"; the quartermaster, standing near, said that it was "because here Jonah swallowed the whale," which showed that he would be none the worse if he were a little more re(a)d. Well, I did not know why. If I ever heard, I certainly had forgotten. While I was writing about the moon and her "man," a few lines back, my wife came running down from the upper deck and told me to look out of the window, "quick!" (I often need a little poking up in that way.)

Here was the answer to the lady's question. We were passing through water which seemed to be mixed with brick dust. The billows rolled up by our ship were billows of pale blood. I never saw such a sight before. I presume we passed through a patch about two miles wide, then we ran into clear water again. On inquiry I find that sometimes these patches of red extend for many miles. Whether they are caused by mineral substances below, or vegetable or animal matter in the water, I cannot say. If we have occasionally during the day billows of blood, we have occasionally during the night billows of fire.

To me one of the most interesting sights is to stand on the deck at night and watch the wondrous play of phosphorescent light as it dances and sparkles on the crests of the waves. One would think the deep to be on fire. How wonderful are the works of God! In wisdom He has made them all; in mercy and condescension, too, for our happiness, even though we have sinned.

RED SEA, *January 24th, 1888.*

SIXTH LETTER.

I BEGIN this letter at Suez. We have had a most delightful voyage—8,316 miles from Melbourne here, and not one hour of bad weather all the way. The officers of the *Massilia* say they have never had such a voyage as this before. We had expected considerable heat before reaching Suez; in this, however, we have been agreeably disappointed. From Perim Island, at the southern entrance to Suez at the extreme north, the length of the Red Sea is 1,230 miles. The navigation of this sea is attended with very great danger, apparently, from the number of wrecks on islands, shoals and sunken rocks all the way up. It is, I believe, especially dangerous for sailing vessels.

Since noon to-day (Friday, 27th) we have been in the Gulf of Suez, and that has enabled us to view all along the southern coast of the Sinai Peninsula. Although the day is a little too hazy for us to make out the mountains separately, yet the group so honored of God is distinctly visible a few miles back from the coast. It would be a strange Christian

MAJESTY AND MEEKNESS.   229

heart that would not be moved by the sight of those wonderful hills where the voice of the thunder and of the trumpet proclaimed the advent of Jehovah to talk face to face with His servant.

Standing on the deck of the steamer, as it were in historic vision, I saw Moses quietly watching his

FINDING OF MOSES.

flock at the foot of one of the loftiest of those distant hills, when he was suddenly startled by the strange sight of a bush on fire, yet not being consumed. Then follows an amazing dialogue, in which the majesty of God and the meekness of the true Christian appear.

Then I saw Moses making his journey back to

Egypt, wondering how it could be that God would lead His people out of bondage by his hand.

Here at Pi-hahiroth and Baal-zephon—both quite near where I now write—I saw the hosts of Israel pitching their tents under Moses' direction, and heard

A COMMON EASTERN SCENE.

the rumbling of the wheels of the war-chariots of Egypt approaching. Then the pillar of fire, the murmuring of the people, and the reassuring words of their leader; then the marching of the captives to liberty, and the hastening of their pursuers to death, for God was fighting for His people, and woe unto them who fight against Him.

And I heard, oh so faintly—because of my dulness of hearing—the refrain of that glorious song which had not yet ceased to re-echo, even through the wide portals of heaven, one thousand five hundred years after, as John tells us: "The Lord is my strength and song, and He is become my salvation. Thy right hand, O Lord, hath dashed in pieces the enemy. Who is like unto thee, O Lord, among the gods? Who is like thee, glorious in holiness, fearful in praises, doing wonders. The Lord shall reign forever and ever."

And then comes the murmuring at Marah and Elim —both places quite near us during the day—and then Sinai with all its glories—glories which are increasing every hour, as truth wins its way among men. There was laid the foundation of practical righteousness. There the true germ of all correct legislation. There was given to humanity the true balance whereby each can weigh himself, and, seeing his deficiency, may come to Christ. There was made known to man as never before the majesty and holiness of God.

What thoughts arise as we look out upon that holy mount! As we looked, dark clouds had once more gathered round about its lofty head. A storm was evidently approaching. Is He angry with us while our polluted lips talk far too flippantly of Him and His great glory? Lo! there is the sign of his mercy.

The sun burst forth again, and one of the most beautiful rainbows I have ever seen was thrown by that same Hand that wrote the law, right across those hills where in olden days He came down to talk to man. O blessed bow of promise! O covenant of

MOSES RECEIVING THE LAW.

grace! O Thou most merciful, teach us Thy law and write it on our hearts.

We dropped anchor in Suez harbor at 11 p.m. (27th), and went ashore at six o'clock next morning. Of all the dilapidated places on earth, this poor old town is

PLOUGHING IN EGYPT.

Semper eadem.

chief. There are evidences of former life and activity, but the docks and storehouses are nearly all in ruins.

Prior to the opening of the canal, this was the great emporium for all goods from the East for shipment up the Mediterranean. From here in the olden times camel-trains, miles in length, did the work now done much more quickly by the railway and the canal. We spent some hours looking about this poor old town. If I must needs go to the penitentiary for five years or live in Suez exclusively for that time, I pray you (as Carlyle would put it) send me not to Suez. We left at 11 a.m. for Cairo, which we reached a little after dark.

Tel-el-Kebir is about half way between the two. This famous battle-ground is, as I take it, just on the dividing line between the land of Goshen and the desert. I am astonished at the fertility of the soil all the way from Tel-el-Kebir to the Valley of the Nile. No one is surprised at the productive power of the Nile valley, for that is replenished every year by the overflow of the river.

When you look at the fertile land, however, beyond the valley, and remember that it has been tilled for 3,000 or 4,000 years, you are surprised at its long continued fertility. We saw luxuriance which would have been creditable to virgin soil in any country.

But, oh, that awful desert through which we passed before we looked upon these green fields! Poor Hebrews! who could blame you for murmuring? Yet even here God's mercy was seen. In some way He manifests Himself to us all if we but seek Him, and He will lead us through severest trials to the Promised Land.

I see that some of the modern maps represent the hosts of Israel as passing the water of the Red Sea at the Bitter Lakes, and not at the Red Sea proper. Whatever some explorers may think, I am thoroughly convinced that the crossing was at Suez.

In going to Cairo by train, we ran all along the south shore of the Bitter Lakes. Nowhere along these shores could it be said that the Hebrews were thoroughly hemmed in, until they were driven as far east as Suez. There they must stop, for the lofty range of hills, extending back from the bold promontory, called by the sailors Mount Attaka, standing right out in the sea, would quite prevent their moving any farther in that direction.

If we look at the distance travelled from Memphis to Elim and beyond, in six weeks (see Exodus xvi. 1), and allow their progress to be twelve miles per day, we shall feel the more certain that they crossed at Suez, and did not take the route marked in some recent (improved?) Bible maps.

MUMMY.

"Perchance that very hand now pinioned flat
 Has hob-nobbed with Pharaoh glass to glass,
Or dropped a penny in Old Homer's hat,
 Or doffed thine own to let Queen Dido pass."

We saw along the railway scores of water-wheels, turned by cows or oxen, for irrigating purposes, precisely as they are represented to have been in the ages long past; and there, too, are the wooden ploughs with no improvement whatever in 3,000 years.

THE PYRAMIDS AND RIVER NILE.

We went, of course, to see the Pyramids and the Sphinx. To me the most remarkable things about those ruins are the immense stones in the temple of the Sphinx. These stones have been quarried out many miles away, and on the other side of the Nile. How they were brought and put in their present position is a mystery to all who see them.

How insignificant is man's mightiest effort! This temple, once the object of royal and princely admiration, for hundreds of years has lain buried beneath nearly forty feet of sand.

Cairo, from which the great Pyramid is nine miles away, is a city of about 350,000 inhabitants. There are signs of new life and activity. Of late there have been a great many new buildings erected, some of which are very fine.

The American Presbyterians have in Cairo a flourishing mission. I addressed a Temperance meeting on Saturday night under the auspices of a major of the British regiment stationed in the city. I preached on Sabbath morning and gave an address to a missionary society composed of young native women.

Dr. Lansing and his brethren, Dr. Watson and Rev. Mr. Harvey, are doing a noble work in Egypt. Some of their converts are thorough workers.

We attended the native service when Brother Harvey preached in Arabic. Many of the congregation, composed almost exclusively of natives, were fine-looking people. The men and women do not sit together, but are separated by a tall partition which

"O Babylon, how art thou fallen!
　Thy fall more dreadful from delay!
　　Thy streets forlorn
　　To wilds shall turn,
Where toads shall pant and vultures prey."
　　　　　　　　—*Oliver Goldsmith.*

runs the whole length of the church. It was to us somewhat amusing to see all the men wearing throughout the entire service the little red (fez) caps.

We visited the Mosque of Mohamed Ali. The tomb of this cruel wretch is within, draped in red. When we went to the door of the mosque at Suez we were asked to remove our boots or we could not go in, so we decided to stay out. Here at Cairo, all that is required of you is to put a pair of "great big" red leather slippers over all. What a nice thing it is to find a religion that can accommodate itself to everybody's convenience! Our feet being shod with an ungainly preparation of Mohammedan goloshes we were permitted to enter into the courts of this rascally prophet, especially when it was remembered that we would liberally backsheesh the guide.

Close by is the tomb of the unfortunate Mamelukes, whom Ali treacherously slaughtered at the feast to which he had invited them.

From present appearances the old backsheesh business is about done. The people of Cairo seem prosperous and happy, in a commercial sense. We saw very little evidence of real poverty and very little begging. The children along the turnpike road from the city to the Pyramids follow your carriage for a mile at a stretch, crying, "Backsheesh, backsheesh!" but the little rascals in most cases were evidently doing it for fun, or for the sake of a few pennies wherewith to

STREET LEADING TO A MOSQUE IN CAIRO.

buy sweetmeats or sugar-cane, so much eaten by all the Arabs.

We frequently noticed them playing, and sometimes could hear them laughing and singing among the trees or on the green near the road, yet when our carriage passed them they stopped their playing almost invariably and took after us with the time-honored cry of their fathers. Woe unto you if you drop a penny to whet their appetite. Then you may expect to hear the cry of the whole pack keeping close to the hind wheels of your vehicle, however rapidly your team may be going.

We left Cairo on the evening of the 30th, and reached Alexandria in about four hours.

ADRIATIC SEA, *February 2nd, 1888.*

SEVENTH LETTER.

WE left Alexandria for Italy on the morning of 31st January. We had intended walking from the ship to the so called "Pompey's Pillar" (though why called so I know not), and breakfasted early for that purpose; but when we got on deck we saw such a crowd of hungry Arabs on the dock wanting to "dragoman" us and "backsheesh" us, that we preferred contenting ourselves with looking at the misnamed pillar from the deck of the ship, rather than have our patience and our purse assailed for the hundredth time by these tormentors.

I think I have a kind heart; I would like, at any rate, to have, and it is something of a comfort to one to think he has; but one must harden it somewhat when he travels in Egypt. The locusts, the cankerworm, the caterpillar, and a good many other *et ceteras*, are thrown into the shade by these pests, who want to guide you, and, of course, to bleed you. So it was a deliverance for us also, as to Israel of old, to get out of Egypt.

Alexandria is a much brighter and more progressive

Could it but speak,
What stories it would tell!

city than I expected to find it. Of course, it is not the city that it was two thousand years ago. Of that city it might be said, as Virgil wrote of the ancient city of his fathers, " *Troja erat*"—Troy *was;* that is, Troy is not now. So may it be said of the ancient

"These temples, palaces and piles stupendous,
Of which the very ruins are tremendous."

city which was where now (or near by) stands Alexandria.

It is supposed that, if extensive excavations were made, there might be found as fine specimens of ancient art and evidences of refinement and civilization as have been of late unearthed at Rome and Pompeii.

We booked for Brindisi, in Italy. The distance is from Alexandria eight hundred and twenty-five miles, much greater than I had supposed. We read the twenty-seventh chapter of the Acts of the Apostles with largely increased interest. Paul and his companions were put by the centurion into a ship which had sailed, like ours, from Alexandria for Italy. We, too, sailed close by (under) Crete, which having passed we got more tossing about in the Adriatic Sea than we had experienced in our voyage of over eight thousand miles from Australia to Egypt; for it was winter, and that means, usually, in Mediterranean and Adriatic waters, very rough weather.

However, we were not fourteen days or nights without seeing either sun or stars; we were not prisoners; we were not exceedingly tossed with a tempest.

I could not but think of the amazing difference generally between the condition of Christians of these days and those who lived in the earlier centuries. If they suffered with Him and for Him, as we know not of, they shall be correspondingly glorified. Some way, in that world to come, they who have suffered most for Him here shall be most highly rewarded. Though we shall not envy in that day those who shall be more gloriously crowned than we, yet we shall regret then that we had not suffered more for Him here, that we might with Him and with them be more abundantly glorified. If, however, there is not the same opportunity for suffering, there is as grand an opportunity for toil; and if we would have that crown for which we hope, we must toil on till our work is done.

I see and feel now as I never did before the wide and numerous doors of opportunity thrown open to all lovers of Jesus and humanity. Oh! for more of the spirit of him who was glad to endure all storms and tempests for the sake of testifying for his Master before Cæsar and his household, as well as to suffer the loss of all things that he might win Christ.

We had a pleasant day's sail along the coast of Greece, sheltered from the north-east wind by lovely and picturesque islands, on some of which were charming residences, hamlets and towns. We sailed into Brindisi on the morning of the 3rd of February. This old town was more flourishing in the days of the emperors than now. It was the southern terminus of the old Appian way. This fact reveals its ancient importance as a port of entry to old Rome.

We were off by the first train for Naples. The train takes you along the Gulf of Venice, as far as

Foggia, which makes that part of the journey very much more interesting than if it were entirely inland.

We passed through many miles of olive groves. The tenacity of life of an olive tree is most remarkable. In many instances the entire body of the tree had decayed with age, and only a shell bore up the living

THE APPIAN WAY.

and fruitful branches. Though thousands of those we saw must have been of great age, we saw none dead. I noticed particularly that the tree flourished in thin and rocky soil, where almost all other fruit-producing trees would certainly fail. What the wheat crop is to Canadians the olive crop is to the inhabitants of Southern Italy.

It was near 11 p.m. when we reached the Hotel du Vesue: "Napoli" (ee). For two or three miles back we kept a sharp look-out for old Vesuvius, but the night was unfavorable to our doing more than seeing the dim outlines of that venerable smoker.

When we looked out of our hotel window the next morning, however, we saw the mountain in all its glory, with great volumes of smoke and steam, like a majestic cloud, slowly rolling from the crater over the sides and off into space. The mountain is so lofty and its lines so sharp that you imagine it, at the farthest, less than two miles from you, while it is in reality nine.

Vesuvius never lays down his pipe for one moment he is such an inveterate smoker. It is only once in a long while, however, that he cleans out his pipe. Friends in Naples told us that some twenty-five years ago, or thereabouts, the fall of soot and ashes in Naples was so great the people had to use umbrellas to protect themselves. Remembering the fate of Pompeii, all those dwelling near feel a degree nervous when these indications show that the mountain is rather more disturbed than usual.

We visited the ruins of Pompeii, of which so much

has been written that one hardly feels like dwelling at length upon it in a letter like this. However, as excavations are still going on, there is some newness to the theme at any date. Only quite recently the workmen found a house in which a lady of wealth had evidently dwelt. She had busied herself with gathering together her silver plate for the purpose of bearing it with her in her flight with others from the storm of fire, but she was too late. Her treasures held her till flight was impossible, and she was buried with hundreds of her neighbors beneath the ruinous eruptions of the volcano.

These ruins reveal wealth, refinement, art, taste, intelligence, which impress the traveller with astonishment. We were much surprised at the durability of the colors used in painting. There are pictures on the walls of Pompeian ruins which are just as bright apparently as when first put on. They certainly had a better art of making durable pictures than is known in modern times. But, alas for them! The very durability of their pictures reveals to us their voluptuous and adulterous wickedness, by reason of which they were destroyed like the wretched dwellers in Sodom and Gomorrah. There are to this day pictures so obscene, and yet so legible, that the rooms containing them are constantly locked, only to be opened by the

PUTEOLI AND SAL FATARA.

guide to men who would look upon them merely with sorrow, and draw from them solemn lessons.

The terrible overthrow of this wicked city and the pictures and inscriptions upon the walls alike testify, "Be sure your sins will find you out."

We vizited Puzzoli, about seven miles in the opposite direction from Naples. This is the spot where Paul landed on Italian soil, and found brethren who desired him to tarry with them for a week. (See Acts xxviii. 13, 14.)

While at Puzzoli (Puteoli) we walked up the hill over a portion of the Appian way to *sal fatara* (sulphur springs), where was, in ancient times, an extensive crater, apparently part of the Vesuvian system. From an opening into the earth at the side of the old crater smoke and steam roll forth incessantly. One hundred yards away from the opening the guide picked up a handful of sand and passed it to us. It was too hot to hold longer than for a moment. A stone of ten pounds in weight, lifted above the head and thrown quickly upon the ground, tells you that you are standing upon the top of a fiery oven, which may possibly cave in with disaster to some travellers. However, we must travel, even though there may be danger, always trusting in the Lord.

We visited the Naples museum, which is said to contain the most varied antique collection in the world. The collection is too great to admit of any definite description here.

We may, in some other form, give a more detailed account of them a little further on. The most interesting of them all to us was the exhibition of the unrolling of the papyrus records taken from the ruins of Herculaneum.

At Puzzoli (Puteoli) we had the privilege of calling on and shaking hands with Rev. F. Sciarelli (Sherellee), the Methodist brother who, with two or three other ministers, completely confounded the priests in the argument respecting Peter's ever having been at Rome at all, much less ever having been Pope. Sciarelli and his colleagues put the priests in so tight a corner that Pius IX. (as will be remembered) gave strict orders that no one was ever again to enter on such discussions.

I preached on Sabbath morning, February 5th, at St. Anna di Palazzo, where the Rev. T. W. S. Jones is pastor. The Wesleyans have here a very fine property, and Mr. Jones is doing a good work among the Italians. Through his very great exertion there is now no debt. The cause is daily growing. I heard at

1 p.m. the Rev. Salvatore Ragghiante (Ragyante), who is called the Father Hyacinthe of Southern Italy. He is a powerful speaker. Very Punshon-like in his build and manner. The Italian language, so musical in itself, when in the mouth of an eloquent orator is almost as pleasant as the chiming of bells. One can listen with delight to an orator like Ragghiante, even when not understanding his words.

In the great reform which is slowly being worked out in Italy this good brother has borne a noble part. At the beginning of the reform movement, ten thousand priests jointly protested against the continuance of the temporal (Papal) power. The time was apparently not yet ripe for their action. Their movement as an organization gradually failed, for the Pope and his conservative adherents were as yet too strong for the protestants.

From the ruins of this organization arose another somewhat similar, though really more advanced in sentiment. This not only protested against the temporal power, but also protested against obligatory confession; against the use of the Latin language in the church service, etc. Some of the members also strongly favored the putting of the Bible into the hands of the people.

The Government sided with the reformers. When they were silenced by the Pope, and suspended from their functions as priests, the Government appointed some of them to civil offices, and in various other ways assisted them, but there came an hour when the Government somewhat relaxed its policy and decided as far as possible to conciliate the Papacy. Then these reformers found themselves between two stools, and of course came to the ground. Some of them recanted, repented, and returned forgiven to their loving father the Pope, but Ragghiante would not yield. Not only too spirited and manly was he to turn to the Pope for forgiveness, but he had been conscientious in all that he had done. For a time the way was dark for him. To cast off all churchism and become a simple preacher of Christ; without any of that loud-sounding and showy ritual to which he had been trained, was too much for him.

God by His Spirit wrought on this noble mind, however, until he was led to see the full simplicity of the Gospel, and he applied to Mr. Jones (with whom he had often conversed, but with whom he could not agree at the first respecting this simplicity of preaching Christ) and he was accepted as a Wesleyan preacher, and he is, as I have intimated, a teacher that needeth not to be ashamed, rightly dividing the Word of truth, and enforcing it with emphasis and spirit upon those who hear him.

In my next I shall notice at greater length the growing divergence between the Italian people and the Papacy.

London, England, *March 15th, 1888.*

EIGHTH LETTER.

WE visited one division of the Catacombs of Rome where, it is said, one million of persons were buried, nearly a hundred thousand of whom died violent deaths, being slain by the cruel hand of persecution,—"overcame by the blood of the Lamb, and by the word of their testimony, loving not their lives unto the death." Many thousands of these were killed in the Catacombs, whither they had fled from the soldiers.

In the Sistine chapel we saw the famous picture of the "Last Judgment," in which Michael Angelo represents a cardinal, who had offended him, in hell with a pair of horns on his head. When the cardinal saw the picture he went to the Pope and told him that the great painter had put him with the lost in hell, and asked the Pope to use his influence with Angelo to take him from that part of the picture and put him somewhere else.

I think, very likely, the cardinal was no greater favorite with the Pope than he was with Angelo, so **he was told that if he was in hell his Holiness could** do nothing for him, as his "jurisdiction extended only to purgatory." So there is the poor cardinal to this day, with his horns and his horrors forever.

ENTRANCE TO CATACOMBS.

It is well for him if he is there only in a picture. I am afraid some of his brethren have not come off so well.

The Sistine chapel is a wonderful exhibition of the

skill of that truly wonderful man, Michael Angelo. Though one of the most ugly men of his time, yet probably no man of his day had a more beautiful spirit, and no man whom this world has ever known possessed a more remarkable and varied genius—poet, sculptor,

A CHAMBER IN THE ROMAN CATACOMBS.

painter, civil engineer and architect, all in one. How one man could design all that is attributed to his inventive genius is more than any ordinary mortal can conceive, to say nothing of the time expended in executing his designs. He must have had many persons working under his supervision and direction.

I presume the amount of thought brought to bear upon the *minutiæ* of a picture such as any one of those upon the ceiling or walls of this celebrated chapel, must be quite equal to, if not surpassing, that of a well-wrought-up poem upon the same subject—chaos, order, light and darkness, the work of the six days; Adam and Eve, the temptation, the fall, the expulsion, the flood, and so on to the great *finale*, the last Judgment—all wrought out with such attention, not only to the chief persons or figures in the plot, but to all minor parts, revealing an intimate knowledge of the artist with the inspired history, and the most profound thought concerning the subject in hand.

The pictures in the Sistine chapel are, however, only a very small part of the famous works of this most distinguished man.

The corridor or gallery in the Vatican, which contains what is called Angelo's Bible, is another monument to his towering genius. Almost every striking incident in the old sacred history is here set forth in the centres and bevelled sides of the panels—Abel's sacrifice, Noah, Abraham and his flocks, the sacrifice of his son, Lot fleeing from Sodom, etc.

The colors in these pictures are apparently much

superior in brightness and durability to any others in the Vatican exhibition. Their freshness is surprising when we remember that it is now very nearly three hundred and fifty years since they were placed upon these panels by this gigantic genius, who has produced the most original and powerful works the modern world has seen.

The pictures of Raphael, who was Angelo's most beloved pupil, are very little inferior to those of his great master; perhaps his works fall short rather in quantity than in quality. This illustrious pupil rose above the horizon when Angelo's course was advancing towards its meridian; but the bright star sank into rest long before his predecessor had finished his work, Michael Angelo having lived to the good old age of eighty-nine.

There is an interesting story told of the great artist's hint to his capable pupil. Raphael had upon his easel a subject; but when he was out the master called. At one glance, Angelo's quick eye saw his pupil's latent power, and at the same time his want of confidence in himself. Taking a bit of chalk he swept a large half circle beneath the picture, and added the word "*Amplius.*" The pupil took the hint, and no longer cramped his genius with foolish, timid modesty. In a few years his name was enrolled with the long list of Italian artists, among whom he and his more illustrious master shine as stars of greater magnitude.

We visited the Pantheon, the shrine of "all the gods," where we found the tombs of Raphael and the first king of Italy. The Pantheon was built by Agrippa, son-in-law to Augustus. It is generally called the "Rotunda," because of its form. It is about 140 feet in diameter and 150 feet in height. The light is admitted only through an opening in the dome. The portico consists of a massive roof resting on sixteen columns of oriental granite, each of which is fifteen feet in circumference. It was, when ancient Rome was at the height of her glory as a heathen city, adorned with bronze and other beautiful statues of all the Roman deities. These were removed by Constantine.

It gives one some idea of the vast changes which have taken place in Rome, to learn that the entrance which is now twelve steps below was, 2,000 years ago, actually twelve steps above, the surface of the ground. Since we were in the ancient city, the Pantheon has been flooded by the overflow of the Tiber.

Rome is very much more modernized than I had expected to find it. The carriages and horses and entire equipage, with the dresses of the better classes of the people seen upon the Corso, are quite up to those seen at Hyde Park and Rotten Row.

There is now very much building going on. There are whole streets of new buildings. I am told that this progress is altogether fictitious, and that before long this apparent progress will be checked, and that bankruptcy and ruin are sure to follow. I have heard that said about so many places, that I attach little weight to such statements. I am glad to see evidences of prosperity, and hope it may prove permanent, now that Rome and Italy are bursting away from a yoke of bondage which in past ages has been grievous to be borne.

York, England, *April, 1888.*

ARCH OF TITUS.

NINTH LETTER.

WE are still at the ancient capital of the world. Here is abundant evidence that the Romans were once rich, powerful, and happy, as worldly things go. These ruins bear testimony on every hand. The Arch of Constantine talks to us still of mighty victories. The Arch of Titus, in its bas-reliefs, tells us of Roman power and of Hebrew humiliation. The very stone talks to us of God's justice and impartiality, sparing not even His own when they provoked His wrath by their repeated sins.

Just as we were entering the Museum on the Palatine Hill we were surprised very agreeably by our musical son from Paris coming on us suddenly, and asking if we were in want of a guide. After being so long and so widely separated, the meeting for a little robbed us of our relish for things antiquated. He had learned from our letters when we expected to reach Rome, and had ventured to come down and find us. After our surprise was over, he joined us in our pleasures over the interesting sights and relics with which Rome abounds.

In the midst of wreck and ruin on every hand, there is in good preservation a representation of the triumphal procession bearing back from Jerusalem, on the shoulders of the conquerors, the holy emblems taken from the temple. The golden candlestick is there, especially prominent. So poor, foolish Israel was robbed of her light, because she esteemed it not,

ROMAN COLISEUM.

groping even unto this day, but finding not the true Light, of which this was the figure. No child of God can stand within this arch and view these chiselled records without sorrow.

And here, too, are the Forum and the Coliseum, which tell us of the pleasures of Rome in her palmy days. What millions of gold have been lavished on these places of amusement! We were astonished at the durability of the walls. One must admire the skill of those old builders who could run up a roofless wall of seventy or eighty feet, and make it stand the storms and earthquake shocks of twenty centuries. Within these galleries 100,000 spectators used to assemble to witness the games and gladiatorial combats in the open space in the centre, or (water having been turned in), naval fights in such real earnest that men were killed for the mere amusement of those who looked on. Here are the lofty ceilings and leaden pipes, and bright pictured walls which gave comfort and elegance to the imperial household.

THE COLISEUM.

BY CLARENCE LUCAS.

Colossal remnant! Vast and mighty ruin;
Thou crumbling echo of great Emperors gone;
Like the vague memory of a glorious dream
Remainest thou. Shadow of vanished splendor,
Thy limpid fountains stifled up with slime,
Thy kingly lion's den a silent cave,
Thy monarch's balcony a bed of weeds,
Thy vast arena green, that oft ran blood.

The brooding owl hoots nightly unmolested.
Where first some trembling maid confessed her love;
The skulking rat his midnight feast engorges
Of refuse on the throne where Cæsar sat.

And where the fiendish tyrant Nero frowned,
A loathsome snake lies coiled in the gloom;
Where golden hair waved in the western wind,
Green rushes quiver in the midnight air.

Where are those valiant youths of ancient Rome,
Who congregated in thy mighty walls?
And where thy merry maidens, dames sedate?
Gone! gone! irrevocably, forever gone!
And on thee—doomed theatre of sin—
Where shone the cruel eyes of old Rome's fairest,
The pale moon gleams on marbled desolation,
And on thy site will beam when thou hast vanished.

Here, too, is the Basilica, where it is probable Paul stood before the Emperor and testified of Christ. We saw the Holy Stairs up which Martin Luther went upon his knees, with the word of the Lord ringing in his ears, "The just shall live by faith." And we saw climbing the same *Sancta Scala* a dozen or more poor deluded souls, vainly thinking thus to cleanse themselves from sin. We were told by the "bill of particulars," a real business-like advertisement, that for each step we ascended on our knees we should get seven years' indulgence.

Two young priests, evidently like ourselves, foreigners, came in and passing us knelt upon the first step, and then having kissed the step, looked up at those ahead of them. Both laughed. One quickly suppressed his, but the other, though covering his face with both hands, fairly shook. As soon as he could control his laughter, both rose and walked away. The others ascending were more devout. O Rome!

I had intended asking some of my Roman Catholic friends in Canada, what would become of those very irreverent young priests who evidently were laughing at the very ridiculous attitude of those above them; but now, when I think of it, their first step on their knees covered that sin and many more, for if one step is sufficient to secure seven years' indulgence, why should they not begin by *indulging* in a good laugh at the whole business. Little did they think that to us outside the rail they were just as ridiculous as those farther up.

We were *fortunate* enough to secure a sheet of health wafers, or rather a kind of postage stamp bearing a picture of the Virgin, the "Madonna of health." If you are afflicted with St. Vitus' dance, which some people call the "magrums," or there is anything very seriously wrong with your "in'ards," as Sidney Smith would say, you roll up into the form of a pill and swallow one of these little stamps, and if you are not all right in a twinkling, you are in duty bound, as a good, obedient child of ignorance and of the

Church, to attribute it to your own lack of faith in the pictured paper pellet. O Rome!

Well, what hope is there that Italy, beautiful Italy, will some day break away from all this superstition, this lie?

We visited the Capitoline Museum, and among the many things there to be seen are wreaths, and busts, pictures, and souvenirs of Garibaldi. That brave Liberator's name and history are evidently dear to the Italians. As I take it, that is one sign that things are not quite what they were in Italy. Then there is Father Curci (Coor-che), a priest with a wonderful amount of influence—a man for whom all the people have much respect, because of his cleverness as a writer and genial disposition as a friend.

Curci translated the New Testament from the original into Italian. Unfortunately his work is too expensive for circulation among the common people. In the preface he asks the question, What will satisfy the present disturbed state of Europe? Will the restoration of the temporal power? He thinks it would not. He thinks that is gone, never to come back. Even if that would quiet Italy, Europe, he says, would not permit it.

He wrote another book soon after, in which he shows up in a very bold way the want of harmony between the Vatican and Christianity. For this he is called to account by the Pope and the Council. He sincerely repents, promising hereafter to be a good and dutiful child; but the book is out and shrewd men have well noted and marked its contents, even if its title be written down in the Index Expurgatorius. His repentance is so genuine that the kind, merciful priest (the true pattern for all Christians) who sits upon the papal chair, forgives his penitent child, and so Curci is free, and so free that he soon comes out with another book quite as bad as its predecessors. Again he is taken to task and again he repents, with such genuine earnestness (*sic semper Jesuitry*) that he is once more forgiven; but the book is out, and shrewd men have noted and marked its contents.

At this moment, people in Italy are looking for still another book from Curci's facile pen. To many in Italy, Curci is a puzzle. They know not what to make of him. Some even think him a Protestant who has chosen this way to get his views into the minds of Italians. I do not think that any one ought to be long puzzled respecting this lively-minded priest. It is simply a hard-fought battle between truth and error in a single mind. Poor Galileo was himself an example. I have no doubt that great man, for the moment, thought perhaps he was wrong. No sooner, however, does he begin to entertain the wrong than out flashes again, like the lightning at midnight, the revelations of truth, and he cannot long resist them, be the consequences what they may. Curci, like Garibaldi, is a sign of the times in Italy.

While we were at Naples, Bovio, one of the members of the House of Deputies at Rome, denounced in strong language the influence of the priests in the schools. He was loudly applauded. Bovio and the applause are a sign of the times.

The Mayor of Rome, who, it seems, has his appointment from the Government, and is, I believe, also a member of the Government, in a very clever and eloquent address congratulated the Pope on the occasion of his jubilee as a priest. In doing so, however, he went a little too far, and said things in reference to the present relationship between the Vatican and the Italians which he should not have said.

Premier Crispi sent for him, and after showing him that he had very imprudently compromised the Government by his address, urged him to resign. The Mayor refused. Crispi called his colleagues together, conferred with them and then went with them to the King, to whom he explained all that had taken place. The upshot was that his Worship was dismissed from office, because he seemed to think more of his "papa" than of his sovereign. This also is a sign of the times.

The Queen, who would really like to be a good Catholic, wrote to the Pope to ask if he would accept a jubilee present from her hand. The answer she got was, that the Pope would be quite willing to receive a present from Margaret of Savoy, but nothing from the "Queen of Italy." Whew! and so there is more fat in the fire. Evidently the loss of the temporal power is a pill the old man cannot swallow, sugar-coat as you may. Seeing he would receive nothing from the "Queen of Italy," the poor old man received nothing from any official, high or low, throughout the whole of Italy. The Italians say, "We have no objections to the Pope as the head of the priesthood, but rule this land he shall not." With them the divorce of Italy from the Vatican is complete and forever.

BLACKBURN, *April, 1888.*

TENTH LETTER.

SINCE leaving Montreal I have preached the Gospel in America, Australia, Asia, Africa, and Europe. Surely I also can say, "The world is my parish." If you look at the names of all the great continents of the world, you will see that four out of the five begin with A and end with A. Curious, isn't it? And all the more so, when we consider that there could have been no agreement between parties that it should be so.

Again, this Europe of ours is the only one of the five which bristles all over with bayonets. I have rechristened her "Arm-mad-ia," or for short, "Armadia," and so have perfected the alliteration, initial and final. Whether in her wisdom she will be pleased to accept the new name, I have my doubts. When she is going to set aside its signification, I know not. I only know it is high time that she did.

I preached in the Presbyterian Church, Florence, for Rev. Mr. McDougall. This mission premises was once the most respectable and popular hotel in

Florence, or even Italy. The paintings upon the ceilings were done by the great Angelo. Here Napoleon I. and Sir Walter Scott have been guests. Mr. McDougall had a hard struggle to gain a foothold, and had in the origin of his mission to venture by faith, single-handed; his efforts have been successful, and his mission is now one of the permanent institutions of this refined and beautiful city, this birthplace of so many distinguished men.

We visited Santa Croce, the Westminster Abbey of Florence, where we saw the tombs of Machiavelli, Michael Angelo, Galileo, and Dante, though, strictly speaking, this last of the four is not a tomb, for Ravenna, where he died, retains the sacred dust of this great Florentine. There the inscription is "*Hic claudor Dantes, patriis extorris ab oris.*"—" Here am I, Dante, laid, shut out from my native shores." Poor Dante! May we not rather say, after all, poor Florentines of that day, who could not appreciate this noble soul. Banished! Driven out by a political party who had outnumbered and outwitted him, his property confiscated; an awful decree pursuing him day by day, " Wheresoever caught to be burnt alive." When afterward the magistrates tried to induce him to return, on condition of his apologising and paying a fine, his lofty spirit, suffering much with its keen consciousness of most unjust and cruel treatment, replies, "If I cannot return without calling myself guilty, I will never return."

Is it not very remarkable that all the greatest blessings have come to humanity by way of the cross? "Crucify him!" or words implying the same, has been a common cry in all ages respecting those who have carried in their being great thoughts and principles which the world sadly needed—blessings which can come to us apparently only by means of the Roman soldier's spear, Smithfield fires, the clanking chains of the Lollard's tower, the bolts and bars of the Bedford jail, or banishments and burnings. Poor Dante!

"We will complain of nothing," says Thomas Carlyle. "A nobler destiny was appointed for him. The great soul of Dante, homeless on earth, made its home more and more in that awful other world. His thoughts brooded on that as the one fact important for him. Florence he might never see; but hell, heaven, *eternity*, he would surely see. What is Florence, and the world, and life, altogether, compared with these? Had all gone right with him (in a worldly sense) he might have been Prior, Podesta, or whatsoever they call it; or Florence might have had another prosperous Lord Mayor, and the world would never have had that most remarkable of all modern books, the *Divina Comedia!*"

Not less illustrous are the names of those whom I have mentioned as entombed in this old church. Not far off is the tower of Galileo, whence the great astronomer made his observations which led the pious sons of "Mother Church" to cry out also concerning him, "Crucify him." Here, too, was born and buried that illustrous man who gave his name to "America."

Among the monuments of this lovely city is the Cathedral, or *Duomo*, which was begun about the year 1300. The grand cupola of the Duomo, so much admired by Michael Angelo, was taken by him as his model for that of St. Peter's at Rome. Very near is the Baptistery, with its beautiful bronze doors, with carvings and figures to represent great scriptural events. The principal one is so perfect and so beautiful as a work of art that Angelo declared it worthy to be a portal of Paradise.

From the Palazzo Vecchio and Ufizzi Gallery we crossed the River Arno by a covered walk, above the bridge, to the Pitti Palace. There are literally thousands of paintings, some done by men whose names are well known, and many by those of lesser talent.

Some have been produced by men of remarkable genius, whose piety was as intense as their love of art. Fra Angelica, whose paintings here and there adorn these venerable walls, never commenced a picture without long fasting and prayer, when he claimed he got his general idea from the Spirit, and nothing could induce him to depart from the ideal impressed upon his mind.

We visited the tombs of the Medici within a chapel connected with the church of San Lorenzo. The chapel of the Medici is an octagon, covered in the interior almost entirely with all manner of precious stones. Here are the most delicate and perfect mosaics which can be found anywhere in the world. The traveller can hardly persuade himself that these beautiful pictures and designs are mosaics till he has made a careful examination of them. What patience! What intense application, not merely for months, but in some cases for years, must have been here! Though the chapel consists of one room, probably not more than sixty feet across it, around which are arranged the tombs, the entire cost of the building and its internal decorations is estimated at £900,000 or $4,500,000.

From Florence we came to Milan, and of course paid a visit to the great cathedral, which, perhaps, for outward decorations, is the finest in the world. This cathedral is, in round numbers, 500 feet long by 300 feet broad. Its tower is 400 feet high. It is adorned by 2,500 statues.

Milan has many beauties worthy of being seen and described, but I have no time or space for these in this letter.

LIVERPOOL, *May 1st, 1888.*

ELEVENTH LETTER.

WE found real winter weather when we reached Switzerland. There had been a very heavy fall of snow just about the time of our leaving Milan, where it came in the form of rain. The avalanches were giving the railways a good deal of trouble, and caused the death of several men. Clearing the track for our train, seven poor fellows were buried up in an avalanche and killed, just at the entrance to St. Gothard tunnel. The passengers on our train, learning of the painful accident, made a collection for the suffering families, which we handed over to the station authorities for distribution among those whose bread-winners had been so suddenly taken from them.

After passing the beautiful Lake Como, along whose pretty shore we ran for several miles, we were obliged to halt at Lugano, and remain there for over twenty-four hours till the track could be cleared for us. In passing through these Alps we are reminded of the saying, " God made the country, man made the town." Nature is still ahead. What tongue or pen can

"ALPS ON ALPS ARISE."

"The mountains of this glorious land
  Are conscious beings to mine eye,
When at the break of day they stand
  Like giants looking through the sky,
To hail the sun's unrisen car
  That gilds the diadems of snow,
While one by one, as star by star,
  Their peaks in ether glow."

adequately describe the glories of these mountains and hills where "Alps on Alps arise."

I had thought after leaving Italy I had seen enough, and was disposed to shut my eyes and rest, but my soul must have died within me if I could not be

THE ALPS.

aroused to enthusiasm by the sights which surround one along every mile of the journey through Switzerland. I presume that the skill of the engineer has been more fully displayed here than anywhere else in the world. I do not see how it could be surpassed. Tunnel and bridge, tunnel and bridge, up and up. We are like the wild goats leaping from crag to crag. Looking down directly below us we saw other roads, one about 150 feet below, and another 100 below that again. I expressed surprise that so many railway lines had been cut through these mountains, but was much more surprised to learn that there was but one line, and that we had just come over the very tracks we saw directly below us. We were going up the mountains as we would ascend a spiral staircase.

Winter has its special charms in the Alps. If one cannot see Switzerland in both seasons, then I presume the summer is preferable, but the beauties of winter are also delightful. From bridges over vast chasms you now and then get a view down the long valleys where the evergreens, gracefully bending under a covering of spotless snow, are interspersed with rocks encased in the same material; light and shadow, crag and chasm, rocks and trees and shrubs alternating. The deep abyss at your feet, the interminable depths in the distance; the soft and mellow blending, the frowning mountain immediately above, all combine to draw forth the soul into admiration of the works of our great Creator.

The snow having prevented us from connecting with the evening express train, we were obliged to remain in Basle on the Rhine one night, much against our will.

We reached Paris on the evening of February 18th. This completes my voyage around the world, having been at Paris two years ago. Wife has one link to make, from Paris to London, when she, too, will have completed the great circle.

Though it is winter, Paris is still the most beautiful city we have seen. The beauty of this wonderful city in the summer season, I have never seen excelled in any part of the world. I know of no grander field for Christian work than here. I preached both morning and evening of Sabbath, Feb. 19th, in Rue Roquepine Wesleyan Church, and lectured on Monday night. We met here some good Methodist Canadian friends, Mr. and Mrs. Starr and family, of Halifax. Though the Wesleyan cause is not large, it is making headway. I think if the dull, monotonous church service were dropped, and a good, lively Methodist preliminary opening service were put in its stead it would be more attractive to all parties.

I find at Paris, as also in Naples and in Italy generally, that more can be done by personal conversation with the people in their houses than by the preaching service, though that also is necessary. The people want to be made to feel that some one cares for them as individuals. They can go by the thousand to the great cathedrals and large, richly ornamented churches and hear preaching enough, such as it is, and yet they can say with David, "No man cared for my soul."

Mrs. Gibson tells me that in their little chapel, at St. Cloud, they have conversions nearly every night, as the result of visiting the homes of the people during the day. How Christian souls must covet cities so beautiful as Paris, and countries so beautiful as France, for the Saviour. Much must yet be done to bring this about.

Just now there is a considerable stir over the Boulanger affair. There can be no doubt the General is popular with his army. He is supposed to aim at being President and by-and-by Dictator. He is said to have the blood of the Napoleons in his veins, as he evidently has the ambition and perseverance of the old Bonaparte in his heart.

It is greatly feared if the good Frederick of Germany should die, Boulanger may succeed in bringing on a war between France and Germany for the recovery of the two provinces lost to France a few years ago. When will war cease from this our poor world! It would be a sad thing to see these nations destroying each other; and yet it would not surprise anyone in Europe if, one of those days, France, now most thoroughly equipped, should purposely pick a quarrel with Germany, and perhaps set all Europe ablaze.

After spending a pleasant week with our son and other dear friends in Paris, we crossed that dreadful channel from Calais to Dover, and reached London February 24th. I see by the papers that a proposition is being made to bridge the Channel. It is only a short time since an Act of Parliament was asked for to charter a company proposing to tunnel it. Some of these days they will propose to balloon it, and then when everything has been suggested they will fall back on the time-honored custom of boating it, even if it does stir up the bile of the restless traveller.

BELFAST, IRELAND, *May 24th, 1888.*

TWELFTH LETTER—LONDON.

ONCE more in the City—the great city of LONDON, or, as the rough countryman calls it, "Lun'un." This great centre of British commerce, civilization and power is not to be measured as we measure other places. To them we by-and-by get accustomed—we know all their streets; we find out every "nook and cranny."

With all objects of interest—"the sights"—we are very familiar, but who can so speak of *Lun'un?* I remember when wife and I first landed in the great city, our objective point was Shoot-up-Hill, Brondesbury. We landed at King's Cross. We asked direction of the employees at the station. "*Brondesbury*, Brondesbury. I seay, Bill, *wares* Brondesbury?" As for Shoot-up-Hill, I might as well have asked him for some cross-roads in Timbuctoo. However, after a little we descended to those lower regions where, amidst clanking of chains and sulphurous fumes and darkness, and terrible din, we come by the underground railway to Brondesbury, in the north, and *go* up "Shoot-up-Hill," to Home Villa, the home of our friend.

Although our host was born and reared in London, and for many years past in business on Leadenhall

THE TOWER OF LONDON.

Street, he cannot trust himself to give us reliable directions to many points which we wished to visit without the aid of a map of the great metropolis.

One reason for this is, some of the places after which we are inquiring, and some of the objects of historic interest which we *must* see, he has never seen himself, and very likely never will see.

When we returned from our visit to the Tower we were talking of what we had seen, especially the Crown of England, and the royal jewels and other emblems and rich ornaments; the nephew of our host, a bright young man of twenty-three, a Londoner all his life, told us that he had never been at the Tower, nor had he any desire to go, and so we proved again

" 'Tis distance lends enchantment to the view."

In the more than two months altogether which I have spent in London I have never been able to get, while in it, any correct idea of the points of the compass. I sometimes get on fairly well if I go by 'bus, but the underground railway never fails to put me wrong, so I long since gave it up for a bad job.

If the founders of London and suburbs could have foreseen the great future of this metropolis they might have done much to simplify it. Now it is almost an interminable maze—a perfect labyrinth.

The difficulty of making straight roads or streets was, as we can easily imagine, very great, when we learn that many of the very best parts of the present suburban London—such as Westminster, Pimlico, Chelsea and Kensington—were almost entirely covered by water, nearly the whole region being low and marshy. Then there were small rivers, tributaries of the Thames, running down through what are now the busiest parts of the city. The Fleet river was navigable up to King's Cross. There were also the Tyburn and the Westbourne, smaller streams, which have long since been replaced by the accumulations of made earth.

The greater part of the district east and south of the river in the neighborhood of Sydenham and Greenwich consisted of marshes or shallow lagoons.

The hilly regions in the neighborhood of Kensington and Notting Hill formed part of a great forest, and St. John's Wood was a dense thicket. Through all these places I have gone, but saw nothing of the little rivers, the marshes, lagoons, or thickets. Through Epping Forest we had a lovely drive with friends in March last (1888), and although it is more lovely than I can describe here, I fancy if our old kings and queens were to come back they would not know it, though once familiar with every square acre of it.

We saw the "Hunting Lodge" of "Good Queen Bess," which in her day was thought far out, now surrounded on all sides with suburban dwellings.

The growth of London is very marvellous. We were at Stratford, which is in the borough of West Ham, Eastern district of London. An old gentleman, manager of the gas works, told us that when he moved into the borough about thirty-five or forty years ago, there were only fifteen thousand; now there are two hundred thousand people.

Then there are a little farther west Forest Gate (Epping Forest) and Leytonstone, which have grown up all within the past few years, and are still growing as rapidly as towns and cities in America. Having lectured in several of these parts of London, I had a good opportunity to study the growth of that great city.

Crooked though the streets may be, we must have a ramble through them. Come on, then; don't waste the time in making yourself look over nice. You can pass all through London streets in the plainest clothes. There are too many people, and they are all too busy, to look very closely at you and me, so we can go along right in the midst of innumerable thousands with almost as little attention paid to us as if we were in a forest.

As we shall have to do a good deal of walking anyway, we had better take the underground railway to Bishopsgate. Being very plain people and not overburdened with means, a third-class ticket will do us very well.

We can walk down Houndsditch, which, by way of

Aldgate, will bring us into Leadenhall Street, where we can call on a very dear old friend, E. Cayford, at 146. He will be very glad to see us, I know. If you have any curiosity to see the real Salvation Army Headquarters we will find them near at hand, where we shall see drums piled up on drums, flutes, fifes, tambourines, cornets, trombones, and so on, thousands on thousands.

If David had to bring the ark again from Kirjath-jearim, I think the first thing he would do would be to send to Brother Booth and buy him out. Of course he wouldn't borrow, for he could not offer to the Lord that which cost him nothing.

We will stroll down Cornhill, only a short walk, and find ourselves in one of the greatest thoroughfares. Turning to the right, we pass the Royal Exchange. Looking up at the gable, you will see in large letters, "The earth is the Lord's, and the fulness thereof."

If we pass on we shall ascend Threadneedle Street. On the other side of it is the "Bank"—the great Bank of England, which never breaks. Just in rear of the Exchange and the Bank the good George Peabody sits enthroned in marble. Directly in front of him, under a canopy, is a woman also in marble, poorly clad, nursing a child, with another at her feet, looking up as if asking for food. These are the poor towards

whom the great philanthropist's soul and money went.
This spot is among those best known in London as
a great centre to which hundreds of 'buses run daily.
From this point you are at no loss for a conveyance

ST. PAUL'S CATHEDRAL.

to almost any part of the city, and it is very wonderful how cheaply you can travel in London as soon as you become familiar with the 'bus lines.

I think we will go down to the other side of the square, and look for a moment at the Mansion House, which is at the disposal of the Lord Mayor for the year he holds the office, whoever he may be. We will, I think, walk along Cheapside, which, of course, is the *dearest* place in all "Lun'un"; and out of Cheapside into St. Paul's Churchyard, as we want to see the greatest Protestant cathedral in the world. We cannot stop long, as we are on an exploring expedition rather than sight-seeing. We turn back into Newgate Stree', and, if you like, turn into Paternoster Row, and, afterwards, also the Square, and take a look at Newgate Prison. We had better take a 'bus now, as we have a long road before us; though, if we had walked, we might have called in for a little while and heard Dr. Joseph Parker, as we are going over Holborn Viaduct. Here you will see one of the finest pieces of mason roadway in the world, worthy of being opened for public traffic by the Queen of England, as it was.

Here you will see a busy street right above another just as busy below. Like two great rivers crossing each other, here are two living streams of men, crossing, recrossing, above, below, thousands, hundreds of thousands, each on his own errand bent—for food, for pleasure, for learning, for errands of sin, for errands of mercy, for hell, for heaven. Oh! what a hurrying on and on—on to eternity all.

Out of the Viaduct into Holborn Circus, into Holborn, into High Holborn, into New Oxford Street, into Old Oxford, having come considerably over a mile in the 'bus. We had better run over for five minutes, and just take a look at the great British Museum, and then walk a few blocks to Bedford Square, to call on dear old Mrs. Margaret Bright Lucas, the acknowledged head of the temperance women of the world.

She is a sister to the Hon. John Bright, and is just as strong-minded as he. When she thought her brother John did not favor the temperance movement as much as he ought, she criticised him, and denounced his action just as strongly as any one.

She is a humble, pious Quakeress, loving God and her race with all her heart.

We will turn back into Oxford Street, and walk to Oxford Circus and on to Hyde Park. I think we had better have a luncheon; so, as we have not much time and must be as economical as possible, we will turn in here where we see steaming sausages in the window. We will get two links, each four or five inches long, hot, right off the griddle, with a very big spoonful of lovely white, mashed potatoes, also hot, for threepence. Then we can get a good roll of white bread and a splendid cup of coffee, each a penny. All for fivepence —ten cents. A dinner good enough for a king, and

THE NELSON COLUMN, TRAFALGAR SQUARE.

better far, I warrant you, than that prince had who burnt the cakes, getting a good round scolding for his sauce into the bargain. To save time we will take a penny 'bus down Park Road to Piccadilly Circus.

As we shall be charged an extra penny if we go beyond the Circus, and as it is only a little way we will walk down Piccadilly and go into St. James' Hall, and hear Mark Guy Pearse preach and Hugh Price Hughes conduct the service.

It is a week-day, but we shall find a good house full encouraging the dear brethren and enjoying the services.

A little farther down is Prince's Hall, where I had the privilege of speaking several times, two years ago, at the great British and Colonial Temperance Congress, where I met those Australians who kindly invited me to their country.

I think now we will walk down into Pall Mall, and perhaps, as it is after one o'clock, we can see Mr. Stead, of the *Pall Mall Gazette.* As usual, before one o'clock he is "invisible," and after one he's out. Like many of these London men, he is too busy to be caught, unless we take the precaution to get an appointment made the day before.

From Pall Mall into Trafalgar Square and Charing Cross. Here is the lofty pillar erected in honor of

England's greatest admiral; and here, crouching at his feet, the mighty lions looking east and west and north and south. How big? Well, I should say, each about forty feet in length. Out of Charing Cross we pass into the Strand. Along the Strand we shall pass many places of which we have read. Here is Exeter Hall; a little way back, Covent Garden, Maiden Lane, Drury Lane and its theatre. A little way back still, and nearer to High Holborn, along which we went in the forenoon, are Lincoln's Inn Fields. As we have strayed a little from the Strand, we will come back by way of Chancery Lane, passing on our way the Royal Courts of Justice, Temple Bar and St. Clement's Church. We are now at the end of the Strand; here Fleet Street begins. We walk down Fleet Street into Ludgate Circus, where, turning a little way down Farringdon Street, we take a look at the great Memorial Hall of the Congregationalists. When we return to the "Circus," we will call, for a few minutes only. on old Professor L. N. Fowler, and let him feel our heads and give us charts. He will tell us whether we are enthusiastic sight-seers or not. He will know, of course, more about us than we know about ourselves, and I'll guarantee he'll "*gie us a gude opinion o' oursel*," too. All right, it's very funny, to say the least of it.

Copyright, 1887.

GREAT BOOK MAKERS. 307

We may run in, if we have time, and take a very hurried look at the great publishing houses of George Routledge & Sons, of Ludgate Hill, and Cassels &

ST. PAUL'S CATHEDRAL—INTERIOR.

Co., of Belle Sauvage Yard. We ought to have called at the *Times* office, and Doctors' Commons, a little to the south; but we can do that some other day.

Ludgate Hill (Street) brings us back to St. Paul's Churchyard.

We were here in the morning, so we will not remain now. We pass the great church on the right and go into Cannon Street, then down Eastcheap into Great Tower Street, which brings us to the Tower of London, of which we have read many a time.

We cannot enter the Tower now, it is too late, and we are very tired, for we have done the hardest day's work we ever did in our lives. We have seen in our round a half million of people and more than ten thousand vehicles. What a conglomeration of carts, carriages, coaches, omnibuses, donkeys, dogs, goats, mules; fishmongers, pedlars, street hawkers, errand boys, sight-seers like ourselves; silks, rags, ladies, beggars, honest toilers for bread, and thieves. Before we go to our lodgings we will run our eye over our path for the day. Are you good at sketching?

Very well, then. Draw on this piece of paper the fore leg of a horse in the act of making a step forward. We began in the morning at the toe, up Leadenhall and Cornhill we went the length of his foot. Up Cheapside, Newgate, Holborn Viaduct, we ascended to reach his knee at Holborn Circus. Up Holborn, High Holborn, New Oxford Street, Old Oxford, reaching his body at Hyde Park, having come nearly

A "BEEF-EATER," OR GUIDE, TOWER OF LONDON.

three miles. Turning off short to the left-hand, down Park Road to Piccadilly and Pall Mall, by way of St. James' Square, we crossed over from the front to the rear of the leg, at the very top of it. We begin our return down by Trafalgar Square, the Strand, Fleet Street, Ludgate Circus, Ludgate Hill, Cannon Street, Eastcheap, which is the fetlock; and going down Great Tower Street, we are descending the hind part of the horse's foot, the two corks in the rear resting upon the Tower of London. We have gone in all about six miles, but we have really done nothing at sight-seeing. We have only explored, opening the way for work. We must another day take several hours to visit St. Paul's; a whole day for the British Museum, and another day for the Tower. We shall want to call at Exeter Hall for an hour or two. We have, in fact, in our round passed scores of places, any one or two of which might well have taken up our entire day.

Having rested over night, I think we will explore again. We shall not be so tired to-night, for we shall do most of our travelling to-day by water. Let us go back to the Tower. We can run in if you like, and take a peep at the real Crown of England, and the royal regalia and jewels; at the stairway, under which are buried the two young princes who were smothered in the

Tower; at the room occupied by Princess Elizabeth while she was a prisoner in the Tower, in the days of Queen Mary, of "bloody" memory; at the axe which smote off the head of Lady Jane Grey, and at the block from which fell the head of Anne Boleyn.

PRINCESS ELIZABETH'S PRISON IN THE BELL TOWER.

Oh! it is only tantalizing to begin without giving the Tower the whole day. Let us hurry on. We will go along Lower Thames Street and see the Custom House, and—oh, whew!—next to that, Billingsgate fishmarket. It is said that *"A rose by any other*

BLOCK AND HEADSMAN'S MASK.

name would smell as sweet." Does the same rule apply to fish?

Take care you don't tread on some of these fishwives' toes, or you will hear some of the plainest talk you ever listened to in your life. Fish? Oh, dear! Fish? Baskets of them, barrels of them, cart-loads, tons, ship-loads of them—dried, salted, smoked! Most of them fresh; but some of them—ugh!—not so fresh. Sturgeon, halibut, cod, flounders, shad, sole, salmon, ling, mackerel, pike, trout, herring—all sorts, all sizes, all shapes, from the ugly jellyfish to the pretty sardine. The quantity of fish brought into London each year is about 135,000 tons!

Come, come; we must not stay here. We will walk as far as Fishmongers' Hall, where we shall see inscribed in stone in large letters outside, that all may read, "ALL WORSHIP BE TO GOD ONLY." How refreshing it is to think of the piety of the founders of the twelve great corporations or companies of London. The Fishmongers' Company dates as far back as 1363. With one or two exceptions only, they all adopted some useful or scriptural motto, such as I have quoted above. Standing directly in front of Fishmongers' Hall, we are at the City end of the great London Bridge.

We will not cross the bridge now, but go down the steps near by to old Swan Pier, and buy tickets for a "thripenny" sail on Father Thames. Our course will be very nearly parallel with our return journey of last evening. O dear! there, we have just missed the boat. Well, never mind, there'll be another in three minutes.

Don't fail to observe and count the bridges over the Thames. London Bridge has every now and then to give up some of his glory to more modern rivals. It is something to set out on our "thripenny" voyage at this grand old historic landmark.

The next bridge is that of the South-Western Railway, over which, almost incessantly, roll the trains into and out of Cannon Street Station. Next to it is Southwark Bridge which, when we have passed, our little steamer calls for passengers at St. Paul's Pier, just below the great St. Paul's Cathedral.

Now we pass under Alexandra Bridge, which has four railway tracks, and over which sometimes four trains are passing at the same time, and there is scarcely a moment in which at least one train is not passing over. Next to it is Blackfriar's Bridge; after passing it we halt at Temple Pier, just below Temple Bar, which we saw last evening on Fleet Street, and also quite near Temple Gardens. We stop again at Waterloo Pier, immediately in front of Somerset House.

We are now sailing along the great Thames Em-

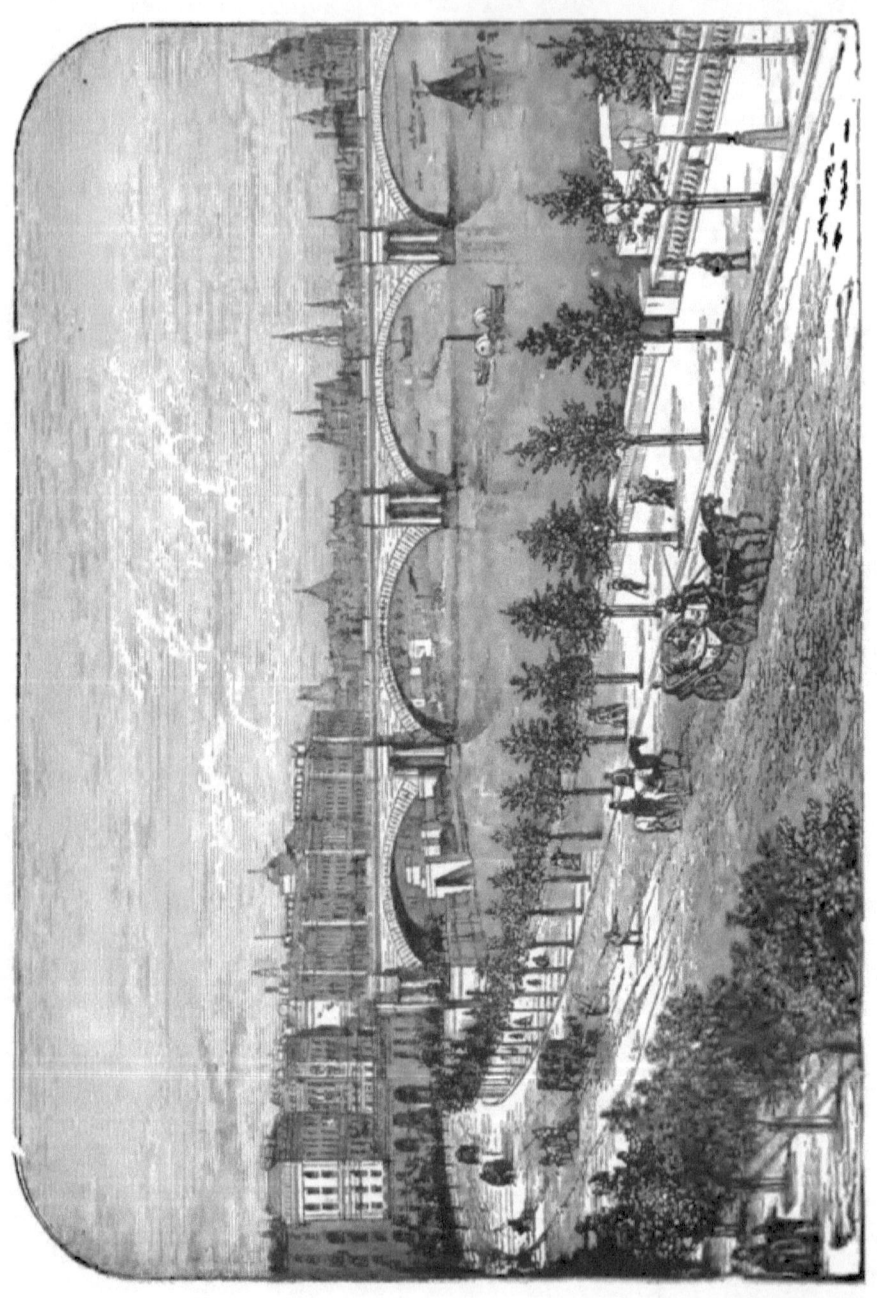

bankment; and it would never do for us to pass it without special notice. Its marine wall of great chiselled granite blocks supports, on the north side of the river, a broad thoroughfare, which forms one of the most pleasant promenades in London. The total cost of the embankment was over £3,000,000 sterling, or $15,000,000.

We next pass Waterloo Bridge, which is second in cost of erection to the present London Bridge, the former costing £1,000,000 sterling, the latter nearly one and a half millions. Let us look for a moment or two at the enormous traffic over these bridges. Over London Bridge there pass daily, both ways, 157,886 pedestrians and 21,466 vehicles. Over Blackfriar's, 87,134 pedestrians and 14,584 vehicles. Over Southwark Bridge, 30,090 foot passengers and 3,560 vehicles, making, in round numbers for these three bridges only, 275,000 pedestrians and 40,000 vehicles. Past Waterloo Bridge there stands, at the very edge of the Embankment, Cleopatra's Needle, so near that you can read the inscription upon it, if you are up in hieroglyphics. After passing Charing Cross Bridge, by looking up Northumberland Street, we may see again Trafalgar Square and Nelson's Monument, which we visited yesterday.

We have now arrived at a very important part of

London. A little back from the river, fronting on Whitehall, are the Admiralty Buildings, the Horse Guards, the Indian and Foreign Offices, while running into Whitehall are Downing Street and Parliament Street.

Passing under Westminster Bridge we get a full view of the great British Houses of Parliament, where so many laws have been made, wise and otherwise; and where, perhaps, more eloquence and true oratory and wit have been heard than anywhere else on earth.

If we were on shore we would go down and see the place where Guy Fawkes was caught with his fagot and fire ready to destroy the king and his parliament. The place is spoiled by too lavish an expenditure of money beautifying it.

Directly back of the Houses of Parliament is Westminster Abbey, with its royal tombs and historic memories. If we had the time we might go up Great George Street and Bird-Cage Walk, past St. James' Park, and see Buckingham Palace, but our little steamer will not wait. Directly opposite the Houses of Parliament, across the river, and also fronting on it, is St. Thomas' Hospital, consisting of fourteen large buildings all alike, all separate, though standing side by side. A little farther on is the Medical School,

HOUSES OF PARLIAMENT.

right in front of the Palace Gardens, and then Lambeth Palace.

After which we pass Lambeth Bridge, Vauxhall Bridge, Military Stores, the Nine Elms, Victoria and Chelsea Bridges.

This will surely do for our voyage on the Thames for the present. We have made a beginning.

This ground must be gone over, and over, if we would know London, for we have just looked at the outside of buildings which will detain us, when we enter, hours and days.

Now that we have had another good night's rest, we will take a very hurried run into only a few of the parks. As we are tired of the dust and the din we will turn right back from this busy street into the pleasant grove. All things are gone from view but the green grass and the lovely trees, when, presto! we are touched by the magician's wand and whirled through space to a Canadian wood on the banks of the Niagara, and we can hear again so plainly the "rushing and the roaring" of the world's greatest cataract. No, my dear boy, though it thus strikes the ear, it is not a Niagara of waters, but a Niagara of human activities.

This incessant roar comes from the rolling of wheels and the clattering of horses' and human feet upon the hard pavements, the street cries of vegetable and fruit vendors, the shouting of the news-boys—"'Av' a *Toimes,* zur; ounly a pennee-ee"—the cry of the boot-black, the singing of the street-beggars, the scream of the steam-whistle, the ringing of bells, and the heavy roll of railway trains over the bridges, or, perhaps, in the dark passages under your feet. 'Tis the voice, the clatter, the restless unceasing energy of a great multitude; even thousands of thousands, like "the voice of many waters," as John has told us he heard.

St. James' Park contains 80 acres. It was a deer park, bowling-green and tennis court in the times of Henry VIII., but considerably changed, and made into a more general pleasure ground by Charles II.

Hyde Park has 390 acres. It has nine principal gateways, of which Marble Arch is the best known. This noble structure was erected in memory of Lord Nelson at a cost of £80,000, or $400,000, but stood originally near Buckingham Palace. Hyde Park, with its lovely green grass, its bright flowers, its shrubbery, its noble old trees, its beautiful, ornamental lake (the Serpentine), its Rotten Row (*Route en Roi,* the road for the king), its costly equipages, its well-dressed pedestrians, is unsurpassed for brilliancy by any other spot in the three kingdoms.

Regent's Park, in the north-west, contains 470 acres.

It was at one time a hunting ground in the days of Queen Elizabeth.

In Kensington Gardens there are 360 acres.

Battersea Park, 180; Victoria Park, 300; Finsbury Park, 115. Then there are West Ham Park, Hampstead Heath, Blackheath Common, Greenwich Park, Clapham Common, Wormwood Scrubs, Tooting Common, and many others, which we have no time to see. We must, however, go out to Bushy Park and Kew Gardens, a little outside the city. In the gardens we shall see trees from almost every land and clime, growing either in the avenues or green-houses. In the park we shall see hundreds of deer. We shall visit here Hampton Court, which calls up the mournful history of the once great Cardinal Wolsey. At the court we shall find the old grape vine, nearly two feet in thickness at the ground, and bearing nearly a ton and a half of grapes in a season.

Here, too, is the "Maze," into which, if you venture, you will be sure, I hope, to find your way out; and if you give the man in charge twopence he will tell you that he never knew any one to find his way out more successfully. Of course, you are out, and no one could be any more than "out."

You can spend hours inside the rooms of Hampton

Court. It is worth it. When you go for that purpose, take time.

Then we must go out to Windsor Castle for a day—a whole day.

If we could only have the good fortune to go through the Queen's rooms, as wife and I did five years ago. That privilege comes to very few. We were most fortunate in this. We saw in the Castle the Queen's gold plate, £2,000,000 worth in one room. We held in our hands breakfast plates worth $1,000 each.

We were in the silver room, and saw silver worth £400,000, or $2,000,000. There are eight rooms through which the public may be shown at almost any time, and these rooms will occupy all our time during the day. We must visit the Royal stables and see "*All the Queen's horses, and all the Queen's men*" that attend them.

Having returned to the great city after this little outing, we must go to work like those who mean *business*. British Museum, one or two days—a week would be far better. The Tower, at least a day. Westminster Abbey, a day, and more if possible. South Kensington Museum, a week—three weeks if you can spare the time. General Pitts River's collection of aboriginal curiosities ought to engage us for several hours;

WINDSOR CASTLE.

it is directly across the street from the entrance to the South Kensington Museum.

We must also give a few hours to the Natural History Society's building near by. We shall find here a magnificent collection of stuffed birds and animals, and of skeletons of animals and fish, besides an almost endless variety of minerals.

Here we shall see also the "Albert Memorial," one of the most costly and beautiful works of art in all London. It was erected by the Queen in memory of her good husband.

Very near it, across the street, is the great Royal Albert Hall, which seats comfortably 8,000 persons. It is a circular building, erected at the suggestion and, I believe, under the supervision of the Prince Consort. All round about on the outside, just under the eaves, are the following inscriptions, in large letters: "THINE, O LORD, IS THE KINGDOM AND THE POWER AND THE GLORY. ALL THAT ARE IN THE HEAVENS AND THE EARTH ARE THINE. THE HEARTS OF MEN ARE IN THINE HAND." Immediately in rear of it is the Royal College of Music, which is controlled by a Board of Directors, of which the Prince of Wales is Chairman. The College is under the management of Sir George Grove.

We must also visit Madam Tussaud's and see the

THE HANDEL FESTIVAL.

life-like waxwork figures and the Chamber of Horrors; then the great Law Courts and the public libraries; the great collections of pictures and works of ancient, as well as modern, art, and so on, and so on. There are hosts of suburbs which I have not named at all, where we shall find many places and things with historic interest.

We must visit the Crystal Palace, and if it is the time of the great Handel Musical Festival, I promise you a treat such as you may never have again this side of heaven. We were fortunate in having the privilege of being present on one of these great occasions. There were four thousand trained singers in the choir, and five hundred instruments in the orchestra. There were twenty thousand persons in the audience, among whom were each day some members of the Royal Family.

The Handel Festival, which occurs every three years, is one of the great *fetes* of London. Be sure, when you think of going, to find out, if possible, if it is about the time of this great musical gathering, and fail not to be there.

We shall also want to go to Greenwich and Woolwich, and other places round about the city.

Here in this great Metropolis of Christendom we shall meet some of the noblest men and women that ever trod the soil of mother earth—humble-minded workers for Christ—and oh, what a field for usefulness is theirs! There are hundreds of thousands who are as sheep having no shepherd. There are in London many thousands of men and women as ill-bred, uncouth and ignorant as the most unlettered backwoodsman you ever saw or read of.

Under the direction of the United Kingdom Alliance I lectured one night in the Royal Victoria Hall, at one time the old Victoria Theatre. The men for the most part kept their hats on, and several of them deliberately took out their pipes and lighted them while the services were proceeding.

What a grand work is being done by Dr. Barnardo among this class. I delivered two addresses in the Doctor's "Edinburgh Castle," Burdett Road. I also addressed two thousand persons in the Great Assembly Hall, Mile End Road. This great hall was built and is under the direction of young Charrington, one of the noblest of young Englishmen. He is a son of the big brewer, whose ungodly factory for the making of deadly swill stands only a block or two away. God touched the young man's heart, and he freely gave up all claim on patrimony which might come from such a trade, and devoted his life to the saving of men's souls rather than amass wealth by destroying men, soul and body. What thousands from among these semi-heathen will rise up to bless such men as Dr. Bowman Stephenson, Dr. Barnardo, and young Charrington.

There is still a lower grade than those who are brought under the influence of philanthropic effort—I mean the thieves. There are in London, it is estimated, not less than twenty-five thousand professional thieves. Some of these, while quite beyond the reach of Christian influence, may yet appear respectable enough upon the street. I have often been astonished at the cleverness exercised by these people in the prosecution of their wicked business.

The story is told of Sir Morton Peto, well known as one of the first promoters of our Grand Trunk Railway, one day mysteriously losing his watch. He suspected that it had been stolen, and put into the papers an advertisement: "*Watch Lost!* If any gentleman, who may have found it, will kindly return it to such a street and number, he will receive five pounds reward."

In a day or two a man called, when Sir Morton was at dinner with some friends. He excused himself and went to the door when told that there was a man outside with his watch. "Good morning, Sir Morton. Is this your watch?" "Yes," said Sir Morton, taking it into his hand and putting it into his vest pocket, counting out five sovereigns and handing them to the man. "I should very much like to know how I lost it," said he; "can you tell me?" "Oh, yes," said the man. "Do you remember a dog-fight on such a corner? When you were looking over the shoulders of some persons to see what the disturbance in the street was about, do you remember a man staggering up against you just as I do now?" "I do," said he. "Well," said the man, "that was when you lost your watch. I am much obliged for the five pounds. Good day." Away he went, and Sir Morton returned to his company, to discover, to his astonishment, that the fellow had robbed him again of his watch while showing him how he had done it a few days before.

Some of their slang may be interesting to those not accustomed to hearing it, or seeing it now and then in police court reports: burglary is *breaking a drum;* breaking a square of glass, *starring the glaze,* three years' imprisonment, *a stretch;* six months', *half a stretch;* three months', *a tail piece;* bad money, *sinker;* stolen property, *swag;* stealing lead from a roof, *flying the blue pigeon;* midnight prowlers who rob drunken men, *bug hunters;* entering a house while the family is at church, *dead lurk;* convicted of stealing and sentenced, *in for a vamp;*

hidden from the police, *in lavender;* whipping while in prison, *claws for breakfast;* the condemned cell, *the salt-box.* Many of these poor wretches live in constant dread. Life is to them a great burden. The professional thief is never at rest. Hear what one of them has to say for himself: "Anybody'd think to hear some'n 'em talk, that it's all sugar wi' us coves w'en we're free, and that we'd no sufferin' till we're nabbed by a beak, but such as thinks that 'ere way don't know nothink about us. Take a feller now who is in for gettin' his livin' *on the cross*, and who has got a kid or two and their mother at home. I don't say that's me, but you can fix it that way if you wants to. She's not a thief. Ask her what she knows about me, and she'll tell you that, *wuss* luck, I've got in co wi' sum bad uns, and she wishes I hadn't. She wishes I hadn't, perhaps, not out of any Goody-two-shoes sort o' feelin', but coz she loves me. That's the name of it. We 'aven't got any other name for the feelin', and she can't bear to think that I may be dragged off any hour and given *a stretch*, or even *a half stretch;* and then my feelin's too, and no mistake, day by day, and Sundays too, as well as week days.

"She's not fonder o' me than I am o' her, I'll go bail for that; and as for the kids, and especially for the girl herself, I'd skid a waggon-wheel with my body rather than that her precious skin should be grazed.

"Well, take my word for it, I never go out of a mornin' and the young un says, 'Good-bye dad!' I thinks, says I, ya'as perhaps, it's good-bye for a longer spell than you're dreamin' about, you poor little shaver. And when I get into the street, how long do you think I feels safe? Why only for the straight length of that street—as long as I can see the coast clear.

"I may find a *stopper* at any turnin', or any corner, and when you feels a hand on your collar!! I've often wondered what must be a chap's feelin's when the black cap's pulled over his peepers and old Calcraft's pawin' round his throat to get the rope right. It must be a sight more'n the other feelin', you'll say. Well, if it is, I wonder how the chap manages to hold on till he's let go."

Some of these poor creatures are rescued from this dreadful life by such noble workers as those whose names I have given, but thousands of them go on to the end in their badness and their degradation, evading those who would save them with as much ingenuity as they would evade the policeman. To the end of time, probably, men will find London a world in itself, embracing all grades of society, and all phases of human experience.

www.ingramcontent.com/pod-product-compliance
Lightning Source LLC
Chambersburg PA
CBHW021150230426
43667CB00006B/324